NORFOLK ORIGINS 2

ROADS AND

Other titles in the Norfolk Origins series:

Further details on these titles can be found at
www.poppyland.co.uk
where clicking on the 'Suport and Resources' button
will lead to pages specially compiled to support this title

WARNING
Reference to or representation of a site, track or road
should not be taken as evidence that such a site, track or road
can be seen or may be visited.
In many cases sites are on private land.
Not all Roman roads are rights of way.

NORFOLK ORIGINS 2

Roads and Tracks

Bruce Robinson and Edwin J. Rose

POPPYLAND
PUBLISHING

ISBN 978 0 946148 70 7

Published by Poppyland Publishing, Cromer NR27 9AN

Picture credits
Derek A. Edwards / Norfolk Archaeological Unit: page 37
Mrs D. J. Macarthur: page 55
Mike Page: page 21
Christopher Pipe / Watermark: pages 6, 28, 41, 44, 45, 62 (bottom), 63, 71, 73, 84
Poppyland Collection: page 81
Poppyland Photos: pages 8, 17, 32, 52, 62 (top), 74, 79, 86, 87, 88
Mike Robinson: page 24
Edwin J. Rose: page 50
Jason Semmence: page 82
The Storey Archive: page 78

All line illustrations are by Susan White and Denise Derbyshire
The folding map is by Susan White

Designed and typeset in 9½ on 12 pt Arial by Watermark, Cromer NR27 9HL

Printed by Barnwell's, Aylsham

Contents

Roads continually change to meet changing patterns of use. Here, the narrower road on the left is the old road in use until the 1980s; by its side is the new, wider road created to reduce congestion for traffic between Marsham and Aylsham.

Introduction

Most tracks, lanes and roads are undated and indeed virtually undatable unless precise evidence is discovered *in situ* amid the original footings. Such discoveries are quite rare. Another reason for a dating difficulty is that very few roads have retained their original purpose, and even fewer their original appearance. Instead, most corridors of movement might be better seen as layer upon layer of modification, change of use, abandonment and re-use; in other words, as complex layers wherein dates and origins and uses have become muddled and obscure and are thus often quite meaningless.

The problem may be expressed another way. Is a Neolithic track still a Neolithic track if, after hundreds of years and dozens of modifications, its route is now the line of a trunk road? If so, then the A11 from Norwich to Thetford is not the A11 at all, but a 17th and 18th century turnpike, or maybe even an Iron Age path.

Tracks and roads change, substantially and continually. They arise from an initial need, progress across landscapes and pass landmarks which may no longer exist, or no longer offer clues as to what that original need or purpose was; and once in being, exert an influence and sometimes a character all of their own.

It is a very thick series of layers indeed, and an understanding of this complexity may require a subtle change in attitude and an approach somewhat different from the traditional way in which we look at tracks and roads. This is especially so in relation to the pre-Roman period.

ROADS AND TRACKS

The Icknield Way is one example. The single track-concept – which was often supported by the mapping of the locations of find spots – is nowadays much less tenable. For one thing, it is now known that a study of the distribution of find spots is not necessarily the most accurate way to gather evidence on which to base such opinions. For example, distribution maps give no clue as to what is still waiting to be found, or where those finds might be. They may also give a somewhat distorted picture by merely reflecting different levels of search and study activity in particular locations.

Aside from the tracks and trails of pre-history (and with the exception of engineered Roman roads and some urban projects, no roads or tracks in use before the 18th or 19th century had proper surfaces) the general history of actual construction might usefully be divided into three phases: Roman, Turnpike, and Motorway, or in the case of Norfolk which does not possess a single metre of motorway, Bypass.

It is these comparatively short periods of activity, and the considerably longer periods of inactivity or modification, that we hope to examine in the light of current knowledge and understanding by offering, in this book, a

The roads of the county have generally retained a consistent pattern over the centuries; the demands of the modern dual carriageway have probably produced the most significant changes. Here the A47 near Bawburgh has cut the previous road system and taken substantial land for the provision of slip roads.

sample of the available archaeological evidence.

Therefore, it should be understood at once that ley-line enthusiasts will find little support or comfort here. While it does seem probable that some stones or landmarks (and later, church towers) were used for guidance or as boundary marks, there is no actual evidence that a ley-line system was in common and thus widespread use as a general means of navigation.

The unlikelihood of the existence of such a system can be demonstrated at ground level. In a young piece of woodland at Knettishall (Suffolk) some years ago, strollers began to divert from an established track in order to take a shorter route. Thus two trodden paths quickly became established as walkers dodged around the saplings and young trees. A year later there were so many twists, turns and alternative paths, all leading roughly in the same direction, that the woodland tracks began to resemble the lines at a large railway marshalling yard.

Again, when an existing car park was modernised in a Norfolk market town the authorities saw fit to include in the design a grassed area with formal pedestrian paths. It soon became clear that one particular path was not in the place where the public wanted it. Most pedestrians simply walked over the grass to get to their destination, quickly establishing a number of unofficial and informal paths.

It seems clear that humans (and animals for that matter), left to their own devices, are and have always been much too adaptable, too ingenious, and too impatient to remain trapped within or satisfied by the rigid limitations of straight lines.

Pre-Roman Tracks

About 8,000 B.C. the cold climate of the Late Glacial phase finally and slowly evolved into the milder though still cold conditions of the Mesolithic period. As the ice retreated (it would take 10,000 years for it to reach its present limits) so the melt waters deposited boulders, gravel and silt over a landscape ravaged, crushed and scoured by the huge sheets and now pulled apart by the dramatic effects of the freeze/thaw climate. Inevitably, river and drainage patterns were changed quite dramatically, too. And so the contours of the landscape we find so familar today also begin to emerge. Slowly, too, woodlands of birch and pine replaced the copses of the tundra.

This was at a time when eastern England was still joined to the Continent by the so-called Northsealand bridge, or Doggerland, a vast area of forest, swamp and freshwater pools. Indeed, many hundreds of years were still to pass before Britain finally became an island.

Because of the known sequence of periods of glaciation – which included the Anglian, the Wolstonian, and finally the Devensian – and because of the known and calculated effects of ice and climate on the landscape, it is not unreasonable to suppose that the very oldest tracks in this area can be no more than 10,000 years old. Before that date, the ice sheets would have wiped the landscape clean of the marks of humans.

Even so, none of the oldest tracks have been positively dated to the Mesolithic period. The people of the Early and Late Mesolithic periods were hunter-gatherers who, in the Norfolk area, evidently lived in small communities similar to those perceived at sites such as Kelling Heath (on high, sandy heathland overlooking the Northsealand bridge), Plantation Farm and Peacock's Farm (Shippea Hill), in the fen margins, and on Wensum valley sites at Hellesdon, Sparham and Lyng.

Some of them may have hunted aurochs (wild ox) and deer, and caught fish. What is certain is that the hunter groups were of necessity highly mobile, covering great distances as they followed the game, kept watch on the animal trails and watering places, and moved from one seasonal site to another.

Although the precise relationship between humans and the environment, and the seasonal movements of the game, is still not wholly understood it is appreciated that during the Mesolithic period, as through most pre-Roman periods, these groups knew the landscape well and understood it.

At the same time it is also possible that the overall Mesolithic population was too small and too scattered to have created a sustained network of tracks. Instead, these hunters may simply have wandered at will over the landscape, rather as Bushmen do today. If this is so, then the only real tracks of this period may have been those created 'naturally' by animals.

When settled villages first began to appear in the Neolithic period (which opened about 3,500 B.C.) there undoubtedly developed a need for regular lines of communication, for although hunting practices survived for a long time the gradual development of farming techniques, and the attainment of a farming lifestyle, began to forge stronger links between people and places. It seems to have been at about this time that the first permanent tracks began to appear.

Indeed, what started as a shifting form of agriculture gradually evolved, as forest clearance increased, into a system of developing permanence. There would also have been an increasing degree of purposeful direction, a greater need for systems of tracks to serve settlements, ritual sites, fields, rivers, coastal areas and animals; and a greater need for longer paths for trade.

And tracks are quite easily established. Given regular use, what may have begun as a visible trail through long grass can develop, within several weeks, into a seemingly substantial route.

It is certain that goods – including the products of local flint industries, such as those at Grimes Graves and other mining locations – were traded over long distances. It is less certain they were carried along main trading routes radiating, as some have suggested, from Wiltshire. It is even possible that river and coastal shipping was as important if not more important than the land haulage business.

In any event, the people of the Neolithic period were widespread and the population was expanding, many of them concentrating, as far as the Norfolk area was concerned, along the eastern edge of the fens bordering the surmised line of the Icknield Way.

Norfolk's portion of the Icknield Way was undoubtedly in use during the Neolithic period, but there is little evidence to suggest that it existed locally as a single and continuous track. Indeed, it is unlikely to have done so. Obstructions, diversions, alternating weather conditions, and the need to cross watercourses and different terrains would almost certainly have brought safer, alternative tracks into being at a very early stage.

There is some evidence that between Gayton Thorpe and Grimston the Way had at least one 'all weather' track slightly to the east of a marginally shorter 'summer' track, which is generally followed by the line of the present B1153 road. Both of these routes were close to the spring line, an important resource later utilised by the Romans. On the other hand, an enigmatic enclosure excavated in 1980–82 at Gallows Hill, near Thetford, right on the theoretical line of the Icknield Way, produced no actual evidence of any major trackway.

It is difficult to decide how important the Icknield Way was, or indeed, if it was important at all. It might have been a trading artery. Again, there could have been other more important lines of communication, now completely lost and forgotten.

Whatever the truth of the matter it is clear that by about 2000 B.C., towards the end of the Neolithic period, East Anglia was firmly established as a region of stock breeders and farmers.

Many of the Neolithic tracks would have remained useful throughout the Bronze Age, which saw settlements sometimes develop as small groups of thatched round houses surrounded by palisades set among well ordered and perhaps hedge-lined fields. By now field and track were thoroughly integrated. So, no doubt, were the arteries of trade which saw not only the passing of itinerant smiths but later, and during the Iron Age, the passage of wheeled transport and animals and the haulage of ore, tools, weapons, luxury goods and salt.

Expanding populations and an increasing degree of trade and social order would also have brought increasing sophistication in matters of travel and communication. The landscape was opening out. Iron Age constructions at places like Warham, South Creake, Holkham, Narborough and Thetford testify to a degree of social organisation. Thus many of the tracks and paths of this period were the products not of the wanderings of hunters, but of population and economic growth and development.

At the same time, obstacles and wear and tear from weather, hoof and wheel must have caused the unrepaired tracks to continually disintegrate, and thus divert and 'wander'.

As we explained earlier, surprisingly few of these pre-Roman tracks have been, or can be, dated by archaeological evidence. Thus many claims are dubious. Nevertheless, it is clear that the people of the post-Devensian glaciation period were technically advanced and commercially developed. The tracks and trails which criss-crossed the land must have mirrored these activities.

The Icknield Way

The Icknield Way (numbered **3** on the folding map at the end of this book) may have had its origins in animal migration routes, perhaps about 8,000 B.C. In any event the upper and lower reaches of the chalk ridge of north-west Norfolk seem to have provided a means of communication and to have been a corridor of some significance over a period of many hundreds of years. In terms of the Icknield's pre-Roman appearance, however, it needs to be seen not as a single path striding along the ridge but as a swathe of straggling tracks wandering roughly in the same direction.

Over the years it has provided a great many problems of interpretation, one of the most difficult being the actual direction taken, particularly between Newmarket and Thetford, and north of Thetford. A considerable antiquarian debate has surrounded the subject, but the central theory, that it crossed the river at Nuns' Bridges, where it was guarded by the Iron Age fort, is still pre-eminent. It is also generally accepted that the route then turned north towards Bodney and ran on towards Ringstead and Hunstanton. This is also how the concept of a single track (perhaps running all the way from Wiltshire and the Chilterns to the coast) gained substance.

In the 19th century, however, an alternative line of thought emerged that the route might have headed not towards Ringstead, but by following the line of Green Lane (**35**), to the north of Thetford, towards Norwich. In part, this was linked to an idea current at the time that Norwich was a pre-Roman city, and Green Lane – which might be contemporary with the Way – seems to have provided a convenient peg on which to hang the theory.

Many matters are still unresolved. For example, it is not known for certain if the Way did actually reach the coast. It may have petered out on Ringstead Downs. Also, north of the Nar, the generally accepted line of the corridor would seem to bear little relationship to the distribution of Iron Age finds. Thus another suggestion is that the single track marked on old Ordnance Survey maps may in fact be medieval, even though this line may have been at the heart of the swathe of original Icknield Way tracks.

Some of the Icknield routes, of course, were utilised by the Romans who settled and farmed this portion of the county to a quite considerable extent.

The origin of the name Icknield is not known, but it has been suggested that it may be derived from the Iceni, meaning 'the road leading to their land'. As Norfolk people were referred to as 'Ikenny' as late as the 1950s this seems at least plausible.

A track in the Midlands known as Ryknield Street is believed to take its name from the Icknield Way, as may the villages of Ickleton (Cambs) and Ickleford (Herts).

Tracks

Although Iron Age trackways probably contribute more lines to modern maps than any other human factor, most of them are now undatable and quite unrecognisable. Over the centuries they have been subject to constant modification, re-use and obliteration.

Reconstruction of a pre-Roman trackway. This is how parts of the Icknield Way might have looked.

There are many pieces of track and road (such as Green Bank (**34**), near Ringstead, and Green Lane (**35**), Thetford) which may pre-date the Roman period. Another possibility is a 100-yard fragment of undated trackway between Larlingford and the former airfield at Snetterton (**36**). A somewhat larger example is Norwich Long Lane (**37**) at Fakenham, modified still further a few years ago by the construction of Fakenham bypass. Passing to the north of the town, Norwich Long Lane runs from close to Waterden (the line of a later Roman road) by West Barsham and Lodge Farm, only to peter out near the Saxon cemetery site at Pensthorpe Hall.

One more example is the Harling Drove (**38**). The fen edges have proved exceedingly rich in pre-Roman material, and the Harling Drove road seems to have had its beginnings at Blackdyke, near Hockwold, which was once a dyke leading to the sea. From Hockwold, the line of the road can be traced by Weeting, north of Santon Downham, and roughly as far as the railway line near Bridgham, not far from where it crosses the Roman Peddars Way. It may have progressed further towards East Harling. It would also, of course, have crossed the line of the Icknield Way and gone within a short distance of the Grimes Graves flint mines complex.

The dating of this route is problematical. While it is possible that the Harling Drove road dates from the Neolithic period, and that it was in part altered and improved by the Romans, its origins could equally be medieval. In more recent centuries it is thought to have been used as a drovers' road.

Fords

A widespread pre-Roman use of fords in Norfolk is inferred and presumed, particularly in north–south travel, which is against the general 'grain' of the county's river systems. Most fords were merely broad and shallow places where the trails of men and animals converged, but it follows that a knowledge of them must have been important as a means of moving around the countryside, particularly in an environment of unembanked and unchecked streams, rivers and flood plains.

Because many fords acted as focal points for lines of communication, in turn they also helped to influence the eventual locations of many riverine settlements, including London, Thetford and Norwich. The continued use and importance of crossing places is also suggested in Norfolk by post-Roman settlement names such as Larlingford, Wayford, Thetford, Stanford, Lackford, Billingford, Narford and Sedgeford.

As with tracks, there is great difficulty in actually proving the use of a ford during a particular period. Very few fords have been dated with accuracy. The locations of some fords will also have shifted over the centuries, because river routes and characteristics have changed.

A number of pre-Roman fords are known to have existed on the river Thames, but as far as Norfolk is concerned archaeological evidence of actual prehistoric use is very slight. One possible example is a ford at Narford, which would have been on or near one of the suggested lines of the Icknield Way. It is also close to Iron Age earthworks and shows some evidence of metalling. This may have been a ford in use during the Iron Age; on the other hand, the evidence may merely indicate a Roman re-use of the same crossing place.

Perhaps the best Norfolk example of a ford site is that now occupied by the town of Thetford, which sits astride the rivers Little Ouse and Thet and which, for hundreds of years, has been an important crossing place. Earth-

Harling Drove road

works at Castle Hill also strongly suggest a pre-Roman importance.

Fords were once common, and regular use by travellers and animals must, temporarily at least, have turned the waters black. Most fords were later superseded by bridges. The name Thetford is thought to mean 'people's ford', or 'the ford everybody uses'.

Stones

The suggested use of mark-stones or puddingstones (conglomerates) as sight-lines is not proved and must be treated with suspicion. In any event pre-historic tracks, human and animal, did not maintain a straight line for very long. Rather, they tended to be rambling and improvised.

Norfolk has little local stone other than flint and carstone, but glacial erratics, no doubt left behind by the meltwaters of departing ice, are particularly abundant in some areas because of the sequence of glacial deposits. Some may have been moved from their original position, while a good number (e.g. the Stockton Stone, the Great Stone of Lyng, Harold's Stone at Harleston) have attracted local legends and significance. None, however, has a proved connection with a road.

Large or misshapen stones tend to generate myths. Large stones are also sometimes to be seen dumped at the side of fields, having been ploughed out and removed for safety, while others have been pressed into service as boundary markers and, later, mounting blocks, corner posts (to protect buildings from waggon wheels or vehicles), and gatepost supports.

Roman Roads

In A.D. 43, almost a century after the initial reconnaissance, the Romans under Claudius rapidly conquered the south-eastern portion of the British Isles. They found a landscape very different from that of today, though largely tamed, highly organised, and extensively settled and cultivated.

For example, the Wash ran deeper into the land than it does at present. Most of the fen areas were already there, but again, the marshland zones did not extend quite as far north as they do at present. Except in Breckland, a substantial amount of forest probably survived, too. East and west of Norwich, for example, there were thick woods until at least the late Middle Ages.

The Romans also found a landscape marked and criss-crossed by innumerable tracks. Indeed, much of the Roman army's early exploration, and its initial military thrusts, must have been carried out along existing Bronze Age and Iron Age tracks.

The Icknield Way (**33**) was already of great age (its origins in time being further from the Romans than the Roman period is from us) and doubtless, and in the opinion of the conquerors, in dire need of improvement and repair. In the event, a requirement for proper roads with metalled surfaces was quickly established. The decision to plan such a network no doubt developed with the needs of the military foremost in mind, and work may even have begun within a few weeks of the initial landings.

What is clear is that the decision set in motion what may be described as this country's first great age of road building.

Documentary evidence

One record, in the form of a diagrammatic sketch map, is provided by the Tabula Peutingeriana (the Peutinger Table) the original of which is believed to date from the 3rd century. On the 13th-century copy, which is all that survives, the Roman Empire is drawn on a series of sheets fastened as a long roll. Unfortunately, most of Britain was on the outermost sheet, which is lost, though a small portion of the south and east coastal areas survives. As a map, however, it would appear to be somewhat inaccurate.

A more valuable source of information is the Itinerary of Antoninus (the Antonine Itineraries) of which numbers V and IX pass through this region. Iter IX deals with a route from Venta Icenorum (Caistor St Edmund) to Londinium (London) passing near or through Yoxford, Baylham House, Colchester, Chelmsford and Romford. The listed distance was a total of 127 Roman miles.

A Roman mile was a thousand paces, or about one thousand yards (*mille passum*, hence 'mile').

Part of Iter V relates to a circuitous route from London to Cambridge (Duroliponte) taking in Chelmsford, Colchester, Scole (Villa Faustini), Caistor St Edmund (here called Icinos, which may have been an alternative name for Venta Icenorum) and Icklingham.

Incidentally, if the Romans did actually give names to the roads then none of the names has survived or has been recognised. Some of the names by which we know the roads today date from the late medieval period, while others may be even more recent – probably Victorian – inventions.

Dating

The dating of the construction of each road, and in consequence the actual sequence of construction, is not known. Some construction, particularly of military roads, may have begun immediately following the Claudian invasion. Indeed, I. D. Margary (*Roman Roads in Britain*, 3rd ed. (London: J. Baker, 1973)) argued that in the period of the initial conquest of A.D. 43 'we may consider the road-building effort as starting in the south-east and south of Britain'.

This view, looking north, shows the area immediately south of Denver Sluice, across which ran the Fen Causeway. There is more than one possible route for the Causeway east of Denver but it is generally interpreted as following the first east–west boundary south of the split in the waterways. At this point it runs through an area used for salt production in the Roman period.

Nevertheless, the core period of activity would seem to have been centred around the second half of the 1st century. For example, R. Rainbird Clarke (*East Anglia* (EP Publishing, 1975)) dated the Scole–Caistor St Edmund road (**4**) to about A.D. 70. Again, recent excavations along the line of the Fen Causeway (**8**) indicate it was originally laid out in the 1st century A.D., probably in the reign of Nero; a canal was soon added alongside. It has been suggested that this road was built in response to the rebellion of Boudica, although there is no actual evidence for that.

What is clear is that road construction began very quickly after the invasion. It is probable, therefore, that among the first roads were those leading from the East Kent ports to London. The London–Chelmsford–Colchester road may also have been an early construction, indicating that what subsequently became known as the Pye Road (Baylham House, Scole, Caistor St Edmund) (**4**) followed later as a logical extension. Once Braughing and Great Chesterford had been added to the system then the Icknield Way (**33**) became readily available to the Romans, providing access to the eastern fringes of the fens and the eastern shores of the Wash.

The Peddars Way (**32**), which runs almost parallel with the Icknield Way for much of its journey across Norfolk, may also have been one of the earliest Roman roads, if not the earliest, in the county.

Once the military impetus slowed, other roads and tracks (e.g. to link settlements, administration and trade centres, anchorages and farms) gradually began to appear. For example, an east-west road across Norfolk joining with the Fen Causeway at Denver (**9**), and possibly leading to Caister on Sea, seems to date from the 2nd or 3rd century.

However, until the final withdrawal of Roman forces (about A.D. 425) changing needs and circumstances ensured regular modification and expansion of the system. In addition, settlements and farms generated their own networks of minor roads, tracks and paths.

The workers

The construction of roads, particularly during the initial phase of Roman occupation, was a military responsibility. One reason for this may have been that a planned network of metalled surfaces, allowing for the easy passage of men, animals and materials in all weathers and at the greatest possible speed, was seen as an essential element of a military campaign. As a result, the early surveys of the Norfolk countryside may have been undertaken by surveyors who, even if they were not actually members of the army, were at least attached to military units.

One suggestion is that some of the roads were built as part of a rolling programme of development, the highways being part and parcel of military advances, actually being built as the troops moved forward. Some of the early main roads, such as the Peddars Way (**32**), certainly possess an air of having been built under military supervision, for construction methods and the presumed initial purpose of the road suggest a high degree of military specification.

There is no evidence of any use of forced labour. Although Norfolk was a depressed area in A.D. 61, and for some time after, relations between the native population and the Romans, though regularly strained, nevertheless seem to have been sustained at manageable levels before the Boudican revolt and restored quickly afterwards. However, it is logical to believe that a native work force was employed in some capacity. It is even possible that paid employment on the construction of the roads assisted recovery of the shattered post-revolution economy.

Aside from the main military roads, it is clear that some other routes were less weightily built or were built to 'non-military' specifications. This apparent lack of standardisation in design, materials and method could mean that particular groups, while still under overall supervision, were responsible for particular sections of roads, or particular areas.

Another possibility is that some of the work was turned over to local 'contractors'. Either that, or precise military specifications were not applied, perhaps because major engineering was not required or was not appropriate. Yet another possibility is that designs were amended or modified because of a need for financial economy.

Whatever the correct interpretation, the construction of the county's network of main roads, minor roads, lanes and tracks, a task which must have been spread over many decades, clearly required specialist knowledge, considerable organisation, capital investment, vast amounts of materials, and a large and persistent work force.

Construction methods

It is not known if Roman surveyors and engineers possessed detailed maps, but they quickly gained an intimate knowledge of the landscape. They may also have collected information prior to the invasion from traders who had been active in southern Britain for many decades.

In general, their roads pay careful regard to obstacles, and although not always perfectly straight, display a preference for the shortest practical route. For example, the Peddars Way (**32**), in a distance of about 45 miles, appears to make only one major directional change, at Galley Hill, north-east of East Wretham. There was a Norfolk legend that the Way also turned at Ringstead and ended near St Edmund's Point, Hunstanton, but this story may have been provoked by a side road diverging at this point towards Hunstanton.

The general straightness of Roman roads is also assumed to be a result of careful sighting and surveying from one high point to another or from positions offering wide fields of vision. However, this general concept of straightness may itself be slightly misleading. For example, the Peddars Way today often gives every impression of having been constructed from a series of short straight sections. In some places existing pre-Roman tracks may have been pressed into service, improved and 'Romanised' (e.g. the Icknield Way and possibly the East Harling Drove).

There seem to have been a number of different construction designs and a wide range of used materials. To a major degree the design was dictated by the terrain and by the road's actual purpose (e.g. military, agricultural, local), while the basic rule for building material seems to have been, gener-ally and logically, to use what was available locally. Thus the Peddars Way was a substantial highway compared with the constructional poverty of some of the other roads and tracks in the county.

Interestingly, and despite the reliance on local material, there is rarely any indication of where these materials were obtained. Only a few pits have been found in the vicinity of roads, and none has been discovered in Norfolk.

Visible remains of an agger on the Peddars Way

The surveyors were working in a populated and highly developed land-scape littered with tracks, fields, farms and settlements, although planning permission was something the authorities did not require. So in general, once the line of a road had been decided and measured, and regardless of what stood in its way, a wide belt of land was evidently cleared and prepared. Parallel outer ditches, or markers, perhaps as much as 90 feet (27 m) apart, were sometimes ploughed or dug. In any event, a centre line was marked, perhaps by a single furrow, and the inner core of the road built with materials sometimes scooped from a second line of parallel inner 'ditches' close to the road.

Once the inner core and scoop ditches were completed stones were often used to build up the agger (the actual embankment which carried the road) which was then cambered to assist drainage and 'metalled' with small stones or gravel. Some aggers were anywhere between eight feet and 50 feet (2.4 – 15 m) across, the larger ones presumably for double lines of traffic. Others seem to have been built specifically to improve conditions as the roads approached or crossed wet or boggy areas.

There is a visible example of a short section of faintly discernible agger (private, and marginally overgrown) south of the river Thet at Brettenham, where it forms the western boundary of the Thorpe Woodlands caravan and camping site. Another example, again on the Peddars Way, is north of the woodland belt just to the north of the Brettenham–Bridgham road, where the Way acts as the dividing line between farm fields. Other possible examples north of Shepherd's Bush (near Castle Acre) have become eroded over the years.

Incidentally, this type of embankment gave rise to the term 'high road',

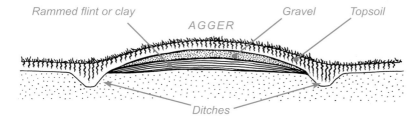

Cross-section of a Roman road, showing the way some of them were built with local materials and then 'metalled' with small stones and gravel. The section also shows the modern outline of subsequent soil deposits and vegetation growth.

Reconstruction of Roman road-building methods. Note the 'sighting' system, and the cleared land on either side.

which later took on the meaning of any road of particular importance.

Many of the local roads or lanes were little more than tracks. Others were more substantial constructions. One section of the Denver road (the Fen Causeway) (**8**) was built on a foundation of oak trunks and branches, wattle, stones, and two to three feet (30–60 cm) of gravel aggregate. On the other hand, when the line of the Peddars Way was cut by excavation equipment prior to the building of the Swaffham bypass, no sign of Roman work, aside from a portion of roadside ditch, was discovered. The road itself had either been destroyed by years of agricultural activity, or the section was originally built without an agger, perhaps because the surface was considered to be sufficiently stable.

Elsewhere, the Peddars Way has left more tangible traces. An archaeo-logical excavation at Brettenham in the 1930s showed that here the road was 16 feet (20.5 m) wide, two feet six inches (76 cm) thick in the centre, and built of rammed flint topped with gravel. On the east side of the road a gravel pavement, or lay-by, continued for a further four feet (1.2 m). This may have been associated with the river crossing, or with a nearby settlement. North of the river Thet the agger was built largely of rammed chalky flint and boulder clay.

Fords

The crossing of water in Norfolk, as elsewhere, was a major problem and a major accomplishment. This was particularly so in north–south travel. For example, even today, between Knettishall (Suffolk) and the village of Thompson, a distance of about ten miles, the Peddars Way crosses three rivers and several streams and marshy areas. Indeed, this particular Roman road still crosses at least ten rivers or watercourses on its 45-mile route across the county.

Initially, and in general, fords were preferred to bridges, largely because they were cheaper to build – even if engineering work was actually required – and because they took much less time to establish. They were also less vulnerable to attack. Nevertheless, several types seem to have been provided, including a few which were paved – to make a sort of underwater causeway – and a few with steps leading to the water.

These may have been relatively rare in Norfolk, because of a basic lack of suitable stone. However, there is a 19th-century account of a 'paved ford' across the river at Scole, though the location is not known. Similarly, there are unconfirmed stories about stone slabs being dredged out of the Bedford rivers where they cross the Fen Causeway. There are also various stories of fords paved with 'stone slabs'. If accurate, then the stones must have been imported.

It is sometimes the case that Roman roads on either side of, or approaching, a river or stream are not in precise alignment with each other or with the present-day ford. There can be numerous reasons, one being that the river may have shifted its course over the centuries; another, that because of changing conditions the position of the best crossing place may also have moved.

Droveway Ford (Brettenham) is one example of an apparent slight misalignment. At Blackwater Ford (Rushford) the Roman engineers may even have built a sort of Z-bend, perhaps to enable the road to approach the ford more easily, or possibly to broaden the width of river bed disturbance caused by

The ford at Letheringsett, the only way to cross the river Glaven from at least medieval times till the bridge was built next to the brewery in the early 19th century. The name of the next village, Glandford, refers either to this or a nearby ford.

traffic crossing the ford and thus reduce damage to the crossing point.

Some fords, of course, would have been more heavily used, and were thus more important than others. The two fords on the Peddars Way – Blackwater Ford and Droveway Ford – have retained their working titles for several hundred years. Dozens of other 'ford' names also survive in the county.

Bridges

Bridges, being expensive and time-consuming to build and to maintain, and presumably vulnerable to attack, seem to have been provided initially only where no alternative was available. Nevertheless, the Romans certainly built some with stone piers and cut-waters, and timber superstructures, though most seem to have decayed during the centuries which followed. Thus comparatively few sites have been positively identified in this country.

One example is on Ermine Street (the Roman road built to link Lincoln and London) where the road crossed the river Nene west of Peterborough, and where stone and timber seems to have been used. In another possible example, at Alfoldean, oak piles were used.

Evidence for Roman bridges in Norfolk is very slight, because there was little or no suitable stone and because timber tends to rot. However, some evidence of an early construction has been found at Downham West. The site was excavated in 1933, and wooden post holes indicated that a bridge had indeed carried the Fen Causeway across what was once a stream and was then, in 1933, a roddon – a silt 'bank', actually the bed of an extinct watercourse left high and dry by the lowering of the surrounding land.

Another possible Norfolk bridge site is Threxton, near Watton, where faint evidence suggests a bridge may have carried the Peddars Way over Watton Brook.

In later centuries the building of bridges became important in order to maintain traffic flows. Bridges also became important as markers of wealth, religious duty, and even progress.

Milestones and stones

Only about one hundred Roman milestones have been found in this country, usually in areas where stone is available or in the vicinity of quarries, most being inscribed with the name of an emperor but not always with a mileage. Some were made in the shape of pillars and a few cut as mounting blocks. One milestone found a mile south of Caster (Cambridgeshire) carried the inscription, 'For the Emperor Caesar Marcus Annius Florianus Pius Invictus Augustus, one mile'. It has been dated to about A.D. 276.

No actual milestones from the Roman period have been definitely identified in Norfolk, or seem to have survived. If any were erected they may have been of timber, with painted inscriptions, and thus would have decayed.

Blomefield, in the 18th century, wrote of a large milestone 'lately to be seen on the Bury Road' at Ickburgh. Also, the name 'Rome Stone' appears near Grimston on a map of 1588, but the details are not known. Again, Tom Martin, the Thetford antiquary, wrote circa 1740: 'An ancient stone at ye runne of water between Threxton and Saham Toney Query what it is?' As this might have been in the middle of the Woodcock Hall (Romano-British) settlement on the Peddars Way, it was clearly a possibility, even though it has now disappeared.

The Cowell Stone, which walkers can still find among the verge grasses on a narrow track a few yards north of the present Swaffham to Marham road, may also have been set up in Roman times. Equally, it could also have been set up at a later date. It may be a post-Roman boundary mark, though it does indicate the place where the east-to-west road crosses the

The Cowell Stone, near Swaffham, which could have been set up in Roman times

Romanised Icknield Way. It also marks parish and Hundred boundaries.

The Cowell Stone itself is a glacial boulder, an erratic, and as such is not particularly rare. As for the origin of the name, it may be derived from the Saxon word 'doule', meaning boundary mark. On the other hand, the name Cowell, or Growell, was recorded as present in nearby Beachamwell in the 13th century.

Mileage

Because of lost and doubtful stretches a precise count of the total length of highways constructed by the Romans in this country is not possible. However, it is estimated that perhaps 10,000 miles of roads were built during a period which may have lasted less than 300 years. In Norfolk, the length of known Roman and Romanised roads and tracks amounts to perhaps 250 miles, while a further 80 miles, at least, seem possible.

The actual original mileage of Roman highways in Britain, and in Norfolk, may have been much higher.

The roads

(Note: The figures in parenthesis refer to the map at the end of this book. The list does not include short sections excavated on sites, many of which may have been local lanes and tracks or even paths leading to places of work or residence.)

Coney Weston to Attleborough (1). The continuation of a road from Ixworth, considered by Ivan Margary to have been built before the Peddars Way. Its route north-east from East Harling is doubtful. The continuation along Haverscroft Street, suggested by Margary, has been disproved by Alan Davison who has shown this road did not exist before the 19th century. The earthwork north-east of Attleborough and parallel with the old Norwich Road, once suggested as an agger, has been excavated but produced no evidence of Roman dating.

Hockwold to Roudham (2). Already mentioned in the pre-Roman section. Known as the East Harling Drove, it is possibly a Romanised trackway which passed through a district in Santon Warren which was probably heavily occupied at the time. It crossed the Icknield Way and the Peddars Way.

Icknield Way (3). Again, a trackway straightened and Romanised. Margary concluded that it entered the area at Lackford, formed the south-east boundary of Elveden Park and continued beyond Thetford to Croxton Park. From there the line went from Mouse Hall to Stanford, Smugglers' Road, Hilborough, Cockley Cley, Narford Hall, East Walton, Gayton Thorpe, Shernbourne and Ringstead Downs. There is no evidence of any course north of Ringstead Downs.

Scole to Caistor St Edmund (4). Evidently known as the Pye Road since the 18th century, the name may derive from an inn called the Magpie at Little Stonham (Suffolk), well-known for its gantry-like timber sign which bridged the width of the A140 road until November 2002, when it was removed because of its deteriorating condition. A replacement sign is now in place. The course of the Roman road more or less followed the present main road to Dunston, except at Dickleburgh. Here, the modern road diverges round the Moor while the Roman road went straight on. In the last century a claim was made that the Roman road crossed a 'crannog', an artificial lake dwelling. Its route near Newton Flotman is also uncertain, but there was a ford near the bridge. Passing through the grounds of Dunston Hall, the road reached the river opposite the west gate of Venta, to which it was connected by a bridge. This was the main Roman route linking Venta with Colchester and London.

Aerial view of Brampton, site of an important Roman east–west trade route.

Peasenhall (to Pulham St Mary?) (5). The route was close to Ubbeston and Fressingfield and south-east of Weybread to the river Waveney. There was a Roman settlement at Needham, so the road may have crossed the river into Norfolk, possibly as far as Pulham St Mary.

Halesworth to Woodton (6). Known as Stone Street, this road may have connected with Yoxford or Dunwich at one end and Venta Icenorum at the other. Its course is followed by a modern road as far as Woodton, but it then diverged to the west side of Brooke Wood. Stone Street is a fairly common name for Roman roads, because in Saxon times they often retained traces of metalling, unlike dirt tracks.

Arminghall to Kirby Bedon (7). Known as Blind Lane in the 16th century, it may have run north-east from Arminghall, south of Bixley Hall and through the grounds of Kirby Bedon Hall. It is possible it originated at Venta and could have served as a connection between Venta and the south bank of the river.

The Fen Causeway (8). This road, crossing the Fens from the direction of Peterborough and March, was laid out in the first century, possibly as a result of Boudica's rebellion. Soon afterwards a canal was constructed alongside it. Later, flooding caused the route to be modified several times during the Roman period, which is why aerial photographs indicate different route lines running side by side. The road passes through Upwell Fen, London Lode and Nordelph. At Denver, which was a Roman salt working complex, it appears to have divided into two routes, one leading to Venta Icenorum (Caistor St Edmund) and one to Wayford Bridge and possibly on to Caister on Sea.

Fen Causeway, branch (9). This seems to have formed one of the branches of the Fen Causeway east of Denver, and led to Wayford Bridge and possibly to Caister on Sea. Excavations at Wayford Bridge in the 1970s revealed a road built of soil topped with cobbles, and through the soil bank a box construction of wooden beams lined by tree stumps. A boat-like structure was dated to about A.D. 210. There are three undated fords at Wayford. West of Smallburgh the course of the road ran through Sloley to Fairstead, through the grounds of Scottow Hall and then to the river Bure. From Brampton it continued to Marsham Heath, crossed the present Norwich–Holt road, and on to Jordan Green, Bawdeswell and Billingford. Stony Lane and Salters Lane carried it by Bittering towards Kempstone and then to Bartholomew's Hills near where, south of Castle Acre, it crossed the Peddars Way. The Fincham Drove led it towards Swaffham Heath, over the Icknield Way (by the Cowell Stone) and on to Downham Market and Denver. It is worth noting that at Brampton the crossroads was staggered, excavation showing that the road did not go straight on. One explanation may be that the east–west road was constructed in sections at different times.

Fen Causeway, branch (10). An east–west route through Watton with a possible branch at the west end towards Clermont House and beyond; otherwise, the second branch of the Fen Causeway route, and quite possibly its major branch, which may have run east from Denver through Threxton and towards Caistor St Edmund (Venta). Alas, comparatively little of it has been found. The present main road through Watton may be part of it, while to the east, at Carbrooke, an earthwork, possibly an agger, continues the line. Recently a cropmark has been discovered of a road leading from the site of a Roman temple at Crownthorpe eastwards towards Venta. In the early 19th century part of a Roman road was recorded on Planet Farm, near Wymondham, and there is a local legend of the 'old Norwich road' being south of the present road at Kett's Oak. These sections could easily have formed one alignment.

Attleborough, east to west (11). An exciting discovery in 1998 was a probable Roman road to the north-east of Attleborough and running east to west. The surviving cropmark joined together the moats at Besthorpe Old Hall and Attleborough Hall. If projected westwards, the road would meet the original end of Bunn's Bank, which may have been constructed as a sub-Roman fortification to block the road. This route may also have originally joined up with the Fen Causeway.

Holkham to Toftrees (12). This road ran south from the coast, beginning close to the site of the Iron Age fort and forming the west boundary of Holkham Park and the Hundred boundary. At Toftrees, it seems to have linked with two other roads leading south-east and south-west across the county.

Toftrees to North Elmham (13). This route ran through Toftrees via Horningtoft, where it was re-used as a manor park boundary, to Billingford. Several other short lengths of road radiate from Toftrees, which is an important Roman site.

Toftrees to North Pickenham (14). The course of the road from Toftrees was through East Raynham and Kempstone to North Pickenham, where it joined the Peddars Way, close to a section of the Way subsequently known as Procession Lane. It was still visible as a mound in the last century when it was known as Walsingham Way. A good piece of agger remains in woods at Lexham Park.

Brisley to King's Lynn (15). A suggested possible Roman road, but some believe its claims are dubious. It would have formed a branch of the main east-west highway. It has been suggested it may have continued as far as Cowbit, near Spalding (Lincolnshire), though this would have entailed a crossing of the old Wash Wellstream estuary.

Norwich, east to west (16). The line of this road has been traced from Bawburgh through Bowthorpe, along what is now Dereham Road and St Andrew's Street, under the cathedral, along Bishopgate, over the Wensum river and up Gas Hill, and then along St. William's Way and on to Thorpe.

Dickleburgh to Tivetshall (17). This road diverged from the Pye Road at Dickleburgh and ran towards a Roman villa at Tivetshall. The modern road follows it from Dickleburgh centre to the first bend, where it diverges from the Pye Road to avoid the Moor.

Billingford to Sparham Hole (18). A possible route diverging from the east–west road, it evidently followed a course from Billingford, by Bylaugh Park and on to Sparham Hole and the river. This route was suggested by the late Tony Gregory. The line past Bawdeswell Heath and Bylaugh Park was still in existence in the 18th century, but the branch to Sparham Hole is evidenced only by parish boundaries.

Other known Roman roads include:

(19) a possible branch from the **Peddars Way** at Ringstead towards Old Hunstanton;

(20) a possible link between the **Peddars Way** and Brancaster;

(21) east–west roads from **Little Barwick** to Egmere, and from Crabbe's Castle through Wighton towards Binham. They may have provided a link between the Peddars War and the Holkham road;

(22) a north–south link from **Brampton** to Thorpe St. Andrew (a Roman riverside settlement site), it followed the route of the modern roads, including Thunder Lane;

(23) a fragment of an east–west road at **Scole,** which may have run on towards the Peddars Way near Brettenham;

(24) a section of road which connected **Gooderstone,** South Pickenham and Ashill, it passed through a gap in the Panworth Ditch earthwork and ran alongside Robin Hood's Garden Roman enclosure. Just west of the latter, another road ran SW–NE for a short distance;

(25) Mattishall (Stone Road) running to the north-west of the village for about half a mile;

(26) a road running north-west from **Caistor St Edmund,** it forms the modern road through Keswick and in the last century was visible as an earthwork continuing to Caistor;

(27) various short stretches running east, south-east and north-east from **Caistor St Edmund;**

(28) a north–south stretch forming a parish boundary at **Upper Stoke,** and in 1590 was also referred to as Stone Street;

(29) a possible north–south road running for a short distance on the west side of **Stanfield;**

(30) a short north–south section east of **Hempnall** at Street Wood.

(31) a straight north–south parish boundary between Old Buckenham and Carleton Rode ending in the Double Banks, which once curved round to join Bunn's Bank, and may thus be another example of a road line converted to a sub-Roman fortification.

Peddars Way (32). The Peddars Way, which forks from the Ixworth road near Stanton Chare and runs for over 45 miles to the north-west Norfolk coast, is the most important, most substantial and best surviving example of a Roman road in Norfolk.

It is considered to be of military – possibly Claudian – proportions, and may have come into being during the twenty-year period A.D. 43 to A.D. 63. Its origi-

Castle Acre from the air. The Roman road (Peddars Way) enters the village (bottom) after crossing the river Nar. It re-emerges (top) to continue across west Norfolk.

nal purpose may have been to assist the inland movement of troops and supplies from anchorages in and around the Wash, and to allow easier access to the eastern edges of the fens and the chalk ridge of north-west Norfolk.

Its seaward termination is thought to have been at or near Holme-next-Sea. The present north end of the Peddars Way (and Norfolk Coast Path) long distance leisure walking route, at Holme, marks the correct course of the original Roman Way as shown on 18th-century maps. The modern road further east, named and signposted as Peddars Way, is an invention of the writer H. J. M. Beloe who believed he had discovered two 'Celtic camps' to which he wished the Peddars Way to go in order to prove his theory that the road was of pre-Roman origin.

The Way rises slowly and gently from below 100 feet (at the Little Ouse and Thet rivers) to just over 350 feet (at Shepherd's Bush, near Castle Acre) before falling again to sea level. The general line of its progress is slightly to the east of and usually higher than the Icknield Way, though towards the northern extremity the two routes do move to within two miles of each other.

Some sections of the Way have been lost so that it is no longer a continuous path, and other sections have been subseqently modified or eroded and changed by centuries of agricultural activity, or, as at Galley Hill, by forestry or military activity. In part, this explains why the present-day Way looks as though it originated from the linking together of many short, straight sections, some of widely different widths and substance. It is possible that different work gangs were also involved.

One short section – north of Harpley Dams, where the land is basically high and dry – gives a faint impression of having been built on an embankment, with a gentle drop on the east side of several feet. On the other hand, as we have said, investigation of a construction site on the A47 near Swaffham, where the Way crossed the modern road, failed to uncover any sign of the actual Roman road surface, though it did uncover one of the roadside ditches. The Way itself may have been destroyed by earlier construction or agricultural work; on the other hand, perhaps the Roman military surveyors decided the surface was sufficiently firm and well drained and that the section required little engineering work.

In general, the Way still offers modern walkers a variety of surfaces ranging from metalled roads, stony farm tracks, grassy lanes, and forest paths of flint and light, chalky soil. In some sections, particularly in the north, it has become almost a hollow way, while in other places – as at Thorpe Farm, near Brettenham – sections of agger are still visible.

About 50 per cent of the Peddars Way still marks various parish boundaries. Suggestions that sections of the Roman Way coincided with pre-Roman tracks cannot be ruled out, but there is no actual archaeological evidence to support the idea.

The Peddars Way is crossed by several other Roman roads, and it is presumed there were connecting roads, lanes and tracks probably branching off in both directions but certainly to the west, towards the Icknield Way.

The road's basic directness and its prevailing feeling of urgency provides continual reminders of its military background, and the present gentle curve at Galley Hill (about 150 feet about sea level) represents the only major change in direction made along its entire length.

This in itself may be misleading, however. Faden's map of Norfolk (1797) suggests this junction of tracks and paths has changed over the years, while Margary has pointed out that slight mounds in the bends of the road (visible in the Forestry Commission plantations) may be traces of agger. In point of fact the agger can be traced in the gardens of the modern houses east of the road. Furrows and mounds are not unusual on forestry land, and can be seen in plantations elsewhere in the vicinity of Galley Hill; but there is little doubt that this is the route of the road.

Whether or not the original reason for the construction of the Peddars Way did evaporate fairly rapidly is not known, but it is clear that settlements of various sizes did eventually develop near the road at places like Stanton Chare (Suffolk), Brettenham, Threxton/Woodcock Hall and Sedgeford/Fring.

It is tempting to suggest they might have developed from regularly spaced posting stations where travellers and horses found rest and nourishment, but the positions of some of them (e.g. Brettenham, Threxton/Woodcock Hall) seem determined by the positions of rivers rather than by any regulation distance. At the same time it is puzzling why Castle Acre, situated on high ground and thus commanding an important crossroads and river crossing, has produced only slight evidence of Roman activity. On the other hand, there is evidence for a very early military fort, and a later cavalry fort, at Woodcock Hall.

It is not known if the Romans had a name for this road. If they did it has not survived, or has not been recognised. The name Peddars Way is probably a late medieval attachment which for some reason has survived in relation to this particular road.

There is some evidence that the name 'peddars way' was little more than a generic label for a footpath, trackway, or even sheepwalk, rather as 'roadway' is an all-embracing label today. The name Peddars Way has certainly been applied to many other Norfolk tracks and paths in the past, including a sheepwalk on Mousehold Heath, Norwich. Another example is a stretch of the Icknield Way in the area of Hilborough, which was referred to as 'Pedderysty alias Saltersty' during the reign of Henry IV. Over the years some short sections of the Way acquired purely local names, such as Ridge Road or Deal Row.

Almost the entire length of the Peddars Way is now included in the Countryside Agency's 93-mile Peddars Way and Norfolk Coast Path national trail, which runs from Knettishall (Suffolk) to Hunstanton and Holme, and then along the coast to Cromer.

Conclusions

Without precise knowledge of the dating and construction sequences of the Roman network it is difficult to reach conclusions as to the original purpose of many of the roads, although it is reasonable to assume that some, built in the years just before or just after the Boudican revolt, were laid down first for military and then for administrative reasons. Thus it could be argued that the Peddars Way, plainly a substantial military road of importance, may have been one of the first Roman roads, if not the first, in the area.

Although there are obvious similarities with the Icknield Way (the line of the Icknield was later developed and improved by the Romans) the Peddars Way is unlikely to have been a mere replacement. These two lines of communication spring from quite different sources and seem to have served totally different purposes. Whereas the line of the Icknield Way kept largely to the lower western slopes of the chalk ridge, and meandered from farm to farm and settlement to settlement, the Peddars Way hugged the generally higher route and was apparently made for fast transport, not for farm carts.

Tracks and paths almost certainly linked the two, but it is more likely the Peddars Way came into being to assist the policing of the area and to facilitate the transit of troops and supplies. If ferry or anchorage facilities were available in the Wash then troops from Lincoln or Colchester, for example, could have been moved quickly north or south, thus avoiding the fens, or rushed into the area in the event of disturbances in the fen areas or the Midlands.

Conversely, men and supplies arriving in the Wash anchorage area could have been sent, using the roads, north to the Lincoln military base by using the Burgh-le-Marsh (near Skegness, in Lincolnshire) road, or south (using the Peddars Way and the Fen Causeway) to another base at Longthorpe (near Peterborough).

It is assumed that a regular military requirement for all Norfolk's Roman roads faded at a comparatively early date. Subsequently, it is easy to visualise the post-Venta Icenorum Pye Road busy with expense-account administrators commuting between Colchester and Caistor St Edmund. At the same time, and during the long years of relative prosperity, it is also possible to visualise the east–west connections (Denver to Smallburgh and on to Venta, and the road through Threxton and Crownthorpe) handling pottery produce from Brampton, farm produce from the West Norfolk farms, salt from Denver and cargoes to and from the coast.

In this context Brampton might be seen as an important crossroads: north to the sea, south to Caistor St Edmund, Colchester and London, west to Water Newton and the Midlands, east to Caister on Sea and the coast. Brampton, in fact, was a busy place with lots of little streets, defensive banks and a ditch, and extensive industrial suburbs.

Turn off the B1150 opposite North Walsham Rugby Club and the lane follows the route of the Roman road which led east from the Brampton potteries.

Other communities also grew beside the roads – a few of them no doubt springing from posting stations, or even from earlier pre-Roman settlements – and it is clear that the landscape soon became a busy patchwork of communities, farmsteads and fields.

The possibility of harbours or anchorages off the Norfolk coast has already been mentioned. The direction of the Peddars Way suggests there may have been landing facilities, or something of the sort, near Holme. If this is so, then the general coastward approach of the Toftrees to Holkham road also suggests a similar coastal purpose. If such facilities did exist then some of the landing places may have been in areas now covered by the sea. This is certainly possible. For example, north of the late Roman 'Fort of the Saxon Shore' at Brancaster is the cropmark, now partially destroyed by the saltmarshes, of an earlier fort on a slightly different alignment.

It is worth noting that the north and north-east areas of Norfolk have so far produced fewer traces of Roman roads than elsewhere, perhaps because it is a landscape which in general coincides with less safe places for anchorages. On the other hand, commercial shipping is thought to have made extensive use of Norfolk's inland rivers and watercourses.

During the centuries of Roman occupation a fully integrated national network of roads – many of them radiating out from London – slowly grew, to link towns, camps, minor centres and agricultural and industrial areas. Beside them there also developed many cross linking and feeder roads, lanes and paths, which served local purposes and which no doubt complemented a pre-existing network of tracks which were old even when the Romans came.

Indeed, many other short lengths of apparent roads have been noted as cropmarks throughout Norfolk, and a few remain as earthworks, but it is not always possible, without excavation, to confirm a Roman date particularly if they do not fit into the known pattern of roads.

The Roman achievement should not be underestimated. They laid down the first pattern of metalled roads, and when they finally departed some 1200 years were to pass before anyone tried anything of the sort again. Even today many of our motor roads still follow routes laid down by the surveyors of Claudius and his successors.

The Medieval System

For several centuries after the collapse of the Roman administrative structure, the Roman roads lay unrepaired and largely untouched, decaying slowly throughout the Saxon and medieval periods. It is presumed the surfaces disintegrated first, followed at length by the bridges. Some of the smaller Roman tracks may have disappeared altogether or become overgrown. In some areas, stone robbing must also have contributed to a general deterioration.

As immigrants and farmers rather than invaders and conquerors, the Saxons lacked the wealth, wider vision and the powerful authority of Rome to do much about the matter. But for them, the state of the roads may have been a minor distraction. They tended to develop small, self-contained communities. So the road patterns changed again, or rather, began to coalesce. Having settled into an existing Iron Age and Romanised landscape, the Saxons were largely content with these unmade roads, and thus only those portions of the old Roman network which fitted the Saxon pattern of life were brought into regular use.

In general, therefore, the roads were allowed to decay because many were no longer relevant. Until the reign of King Alfred, England was divided into a number of self-governing 'countries'. There was no longer any need for a direct road from London to York, for example, or from Exeter to Newcastle. Nor was there any central government to enforce the repair of roads, or to pay for it. In the 20th century it was possible to see a similar situation in those African and Far Eastern countries, once part of foreign empires, which divided into independent states whose transport needs were quite different from those of their former rulers.

Thus many of the early Saxon villages seem to deliberately shun the old Roman roads, being sited some distance away. Perhaps they considered it safer to keep away from routes an invading army would almost certainly follow. In north-west Norfolk, for example, settlements like Fring, Bircham and Great and Little Massingham all seem purposely to ignore the presence of the Peddars Way a few miles to the west.

During the Middle Saxon period, villages tended to cluster around their church, but in the late Saxon and early medieval periods, for some reason, the houses began to drift away to the edges of commons, sometimes leaving the church isolated and sometimes even dividing into two settlements. Nevertheless, these later settlements were linked by tracks that may have begun as driftways for cattle. Indeed, some village 'back lanes' may have started life as driftways at a time when stock was driven to fields and commons.

Towards the end of the Saxon period, as trade again took on a wider aspect, villages began to grow beside the roads once more. However, it is clear that throughout the Middle Ages (other than in walled towns, or particularly important short stretches of road or stretches under particular patronage) new routes were not built purposely and directly from A to B. Instead, routes came into being as and when they were needed, and abandoned when circumstances changed.

The period also saw the use of uncultivated strips to delineate fields. In time, the tracks along these grass strips became more or less permanent.

Bennington's Lane started as an uncultivated strip marking the boundary between the parishes of Aylmerton and East Beckham, and is little more than that today.

A right-angle bend in a lane near Blickling as it skirts the field boundary.

This is one reason why bends can sometimes be found in roads which tend to follow parish boundaries.

At this stage the cost of maintaining local tracks was still a local responsibility, and it was because of the implied importance of the boundaries, and the cost of maintaining them, that the ceremony of 'beating the bounds' became of such significance. Older generations may recall 'beating the bounds' ceremonies, or processions, many of which survived to the Second World War, or shortly after, and a few of which linger on today or have been revived.

One of the reasons the ceremonies came into being was to impress upon community memory exactly where the parish boundaries were. Such ceremonies must once have been widespread. One such section of parish boundary which seems to echo these progressions is a stretch of the Peddars Way which runs north from North Pickenham towards the A47 main trunk road, close to the Swaffham bypass roundabout, and which became known as Sessions or Procession Lane.

It would be a mistake to conclude that travel at this time was restricted, unfashionable or even unnecessary. For the ordinary peasant labourer this may have been the case, but changes were on the horizon. The eventual

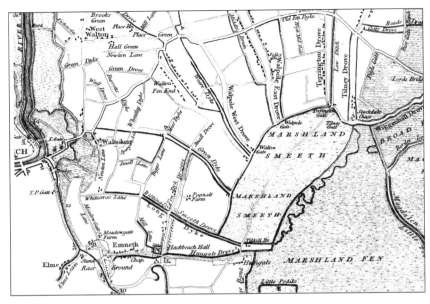

Faden's map of Norfolk shows drove roads leading to the common green. Today Marshland Smeeth is the green whilst the parish of Marshland St James is an amalgam of the droving areas.

granting of fairs and markets, the gradual proliferation of abbeys and monasteries and the burgeoning sporting interests of the nobles all gave impetus to the concept of travel, particularly in the 12th and 13th centuries.

Bartering and selling at strategic places, such as crossroads or even the paved central forum of Venta Icenorum, had been going on for centuries, but there gradually developed a tradition that whereas markets were held at regular places on regular dates, fairs were perhaps twice-yearly seasonal events. They were big events, too. Farmers brought their cattle, the locals their produce and goods, and people from remote hamlets walked in to take a break from the humdrum, enjoy entertainment, pass on the news and obtain their food, goods and clothing. Unsurprisingly, buyers, sellers and trinkets salesmen flooded in, too.

In the fen areas around the Wash, drove roads and systems related to the movement of cattle had slowly developed from about 2000 B.C. onwards. On lands on the east bank of the old estuary between Wisbech and King's

Lynn, and hand in glove with reclamation and improvements to flood defences, linear settlements continued to spread along the wide access droves. One example is Marshland, where seven droves once linked the main villages to a common grazing marsh.

The Normans laid out planned urban developments at Norwich – in the process moving the old Saxon market from Tombland to its present site, closer to the castle – and at Castle Rising, Castle Acre and New Buckenham. But between the mid-12th and the mid-14th centuries dozens of markets appeared all over Norfolk. It was nothing less than a commercial and cultural revolution. Not all of the markets lasted very long, but the most successful helped reshape the pattern of local settlement.

This helps to explain why, at the beginning of the medieval period, travel on English roads proceeded apace with apparently little complaint as to the condition of the surfaces; and why, towards the end of the period, the level of general dissatisfaction was beginning to rise. In essence, the demand for better travelling conditions was driven by increasing trade and industry and an increasingly mobile population.

The English medieval period certainly marked phases of growth, albeit not continuous, in population and trade and economic life in general, and roads still formed the backbone of the system. But the nature of these 'new' medieval roads also began to change. No longer could they be seen – as in Roman and in modern times – as a thin strips of land with boundaries, but rather as public rights of way with legal and customary status, leading from one settlement to the next.

Busy and consistently used routes clearly became physical tracks, but there were important differences between this and the Roman system. First, if a route became obstructed or impassable, perhaps because of wet weather, mud or potholes, then the traveller could diverge from the road on to neighbouring private land, even if it was cropped. This right was enshrined in the Statute of Winchester in 1285. Second, if a route had to climb a hill or bank, then multiple routes were allowed to develop, leaving the traveller to select the easiest or most convenient at the time.

Another edict laid down that highways connecting market towns should be widened so that there was no ditch, undergrowth or tree in which a mischief-maker might lurk within 200 feet of either side (great oaks and beeches excluded). Roads under the king's protection were already supposed to be wide enough for the passing of two waggons.

The amount of travelling, particularly by kings and their courts, was considerable. For example, during the reign of King John, when there was no fixed place of parliament or permanent seat of residence, government was where the king happened to be at the time. In effect, his constant journeying, together with his sprawling household, created a sort of national capital on the move, a long baggage train of horses, waggons, clerks, carts, soldiers, tents and members of the royal household, as well as the written paraphernalia of government.

Slow and difficult though it must have been, travel also went on throughout the winter months. One brief example of John's itinerary, in 1216, shortly before and just after the episode when his baggage train foundered during a crossing of the Wellstream (the old Wash estuary), helps to illustrate the degree of movement he could attain. On 5th October he was in Boston (Lincolnshire), and on 9th October he reached King's Lynn. He was in Lynn on 11th October, Wisbech and Swineshead on 12th October, Sleaford on 14th and 15th October and Newark on 16th October. By this time he was dying, but it clearly demonstrates that movement over the roads, even during the wet months, was possible.

Edward I (just like John and Edward II) was another great traveller who averaged nine moves a month throughout his reign. In January 1300, he covered 360 miles from Bamburgh to Windsor in 25 days, including six rest days. Of course, laden waggons and carts, pulled by horses or even oxen, could only manage a speed of something akin to walking pace, suggesting that royal baggage trains either set off before the main party or caught up with them later.

One description of a medieval route from London to Norwich hints that travellers, on reaching Newmarket, were faced with three continuation options – the present A11 via Barton Mills; Kennett, Herringswell, Tuddenham (Suffolk) and Temple Bridge; or along the line of the present A45 to Cavenham and then to Icklingham or Lackford.

Travelling across Breckland, some of the routes evidently converged at Thetford, where three more options became available – the present A11; a route via Bridgham; and a third route by East Wretham. They all converged at or near Attleborough before proceeding to Norwich. In 1600 Will Kempe, during his nine-day Morris dance from London to Norwich, chose a route from Thetford through the Rockland hamlets and Hingham, apparently avoiding Attleborough altogether.

But troubles persisted, and by about 1580 the number of complaints was rising rapidly. One possible reason was the dissolution of the monasteries which, some think, brought to an end what little road maintenance there had been. However, it is more likely that the real reason was the rapid growth of the later Tudor economy.

Quite simply, the volume of traffic was growing while the cumulative effects of inclement weather, negligible drainage and poor and often unrepaired surfaces is best left to the imagination. The winding lanes were clearly in an appalling state, particularly in winter; and worse, they were beginning to prove utterly unsuitable for a world in which trade and travel were on the increase.

Something had to be done. Meanwhile, the medieval roads and their users must have presented an extraordinary sight. Minstrels, messengers, vaga-bonds, merchants, preachers, friars, pardoners, pilgrims, travelling justices of the peace, revenue collectors, horsemen, drovers, packmen, pedlars, charlatans, the landless and the workless. A jostling, passing parade, col-ourful, bawdy and squalid.

Bridges

Some Roman bridges, particularly those with stone piers and cut-waters and timber superstructures, may well have survived for a time, but it is likely most of them, including the larger structures, had largely decayed by the time of the Norman Conquest. However, thanks to the increasing influence of the church and the economic importance of the markets, a transition from ford to wooden bridge, and from wooden to stone bridge, finally got under way.

The transition was slow because medieval reaction to the need for and the construction of stone bridges was often very mixed. Some notable families and parochial authorities were reluctant to bear the costs, though some guilds, fraternities and wealthy benefactors did subscribe. One reason may have been that bridges often provoked acrimonious disputes, most usually over the critical question of maintenance.

The bridge at Walsingham looks like a packhorse bridge – but can it be?

It was held that the Common Law of England required that whoever built a bridge was also responsible for its good repair. The arguments were often further bedevilled by boundary disputes. Sometimes the administrative boundary ran down the centre of the stream in question.

Nevertheless, a great many bridges were built, often by these same benevolent individuals or religious institutions. One useful answer to the problem of cost and upkeep was to designate bridge construction and maintenance as 'pious and meritorious works before God'. One Norfolk example of this is St Olave's Bridge, the original of which was built as a religious offering by the wife of Sir James Hobart, Chancellor to Henry VII. Sir James, in turn, built Loddon church.

By A.D. 1300 it is thought that Norwich had five bridges over the river Wensum, perhaps reflecting the importance of the city as a commercial, religious and administrative centre. Bishop Bridge is one example of a medieval bridge, one of the oldest in the country, but it is not typical because it was originally built as part of the city defences and once had a defensive gate.

Wiveton bridge, at the landward end of the former maritime estuary, which once included the ports of Cley and Blakeney, is a Late Medieval survivor. There is also a somewhat unusual bridge in the grounds of Walsingham Priory. It looks like a packhorse bridge, but this cannot be so because its present location was, in the 19th century, actually beneath a lake. Thus it may have been moved from elsewhere; one suggestion has been that it is a recon-struction of the bridge that once carried the precinct wall over the river.

Pilgrim tracks

Very few roads and tracks are thought to have been developed for a single specific purpose. For example, there are no known use-specific salt roads in Norfolk. The same point has to be made about pilgrim roads and tracks. One of the best known in the country is the Pilgrims' Way, leading from Win-chester to Canterbury, a prehistoric route which acquired its present name because there was no other way for the pilgrims to go. The same is not the case as far as the Walsingham Way is concerned.

Pilgrimages may have sprung from a 4th-century acceptance of the cults of saints and the veneration of relics, and they duly became a quite remark-able and widespread preoccupation, stretching across Britain and Europe to the Holy Land. At any time during the Middle Ages the amount of 'traffic' generated by pilgrims was considerable, which in turn led to a need for lodgings and hospices. In this way, it is thought, the post-Roman concept of inns developed.

As far as Walsingham is concerned there is little evidence, other than an oral tradition, to support the single-track concept. It seems more likely that in Norfolk almost every village had its 'Walsingham Way' or 'Pilgrim Way', because almost every village had a road along which pilgrims, arriving from all points of the compass, would pass on their journey to and from Walsingham.

A modern comparison of this would be to point out that almost every village in East Norfolk has a Yarmouth Road; but if the phrase 'Yarmouth Road' is used in isolation then it is usually understood to mean the A47. In much the same way, some pilgrim routes – for example, Mount Ephraim, near Weeting – were busier and perhaps more important than others, and were marked with stones or crosses. However, although fragments of pilgrim roads and Pilgrim Ways do remain, they do not necessarily constitute a continuous path.

In addition to Walsingham, which developed into an international pilgrimage centre before the 16th century, Norfolk was also home to Bromholm, near Bacton, a small Cluniac community established in 1113 which was revitalised in 1223 when it obtained what were claimed as two pieces of the True Cross. The relics disappeared in 1537, whereupon Bromholm went into steep decline.

At Paston is found visible evidence of the earliest Norfolk road dispute for which written evidence survives. The church's entrance and lychgate are on the south side; the road is now on the north side, after being rerouted by the Paston family. Agnes Paston, writing in 1445, reports a dispute between the vicar and her husband William the previous year over the moving of the road. Six years later she writes again to her son that a wall built to establish a garden or field to the south of the church has been knocked down by villagers trying to maintain the old track.

The Turnpike Age

For a long time the condition of England's roads and tracks was very poor indeed. For example, by about 1600 the Bury St Edmunds to Thetford road was said to be little more than a track across a sandy heath, and one hundred and fifty years later there had not been much improvement. The way between Thetford and Brandon was still a sandy waste which brought great discomfort to travellers. As for the road at Bawsey Bottom, on the present B1145 between King's Lynn and Gayton, it was said by some to be the worst in all England in winter. Even the unusual name Pudding Norton, a hamlet near Fakenham, probably derives from the lamentable state of its adjacent roads.

Nevertheless, Norfolk's roads are still thought to have been generally better than many others elsewhere in the country.

The problem revolved around the lack of an overall policy, a shortage of firm surfaces, and an almost complete lack of proper and regular repairs. As a consequence, many landowners came to regard as a curse those long distance travellers who, because of the conditions, were forced to stray or detour from the roads in order to avoid difficult or impassable areas. Among these 'travellers', of course, were droves of cattle, horses, haulage waggons, and possibly – though the actual extent of this transportation system is unknown – strings of packhorses.

In other areas (London, St Albans, Hertford and Cambridge), stagecoaches were also beginning to put in an appearance, but the speed of the early vehicles was very poor, and probably not more than four or five miles an hour. Their progress would have been even slower in winter. It was becoming increasingly apparent that the volume of traffic was rising at the same time as the condition of the roads was worsening.

In 1555 a new Highways Act attempted to change things. It provided that two parishioners should be elected annually at a parish session, to act as highway surveyors to inspect roads and bridges three times a year and to report deficiencies. It also ordered that every person holding land of an annual value of £50 or more was required to provide two men, a team of horses or oxen, tools and implements, to work on the repair of highways for eight hours on four consecutive days each year.

For obvious reasons, the Act was unpopular. It was not entirely successful, either. The landowners perceived the duty as an imposition; and worse, the Act itself failed to specify standards or offer incentives.

Harrison's *Description* (1577–86) showed the main local thoroughfares of this period as London–Ware–Walsingham and London–Colchester–Yarmouth. However, it gives a far from complete picture. In 1635, Jacob van Langeren's *Direction for the English Traviller Northfolke* included a distance/mileage chart for 26 Norfolk towns and villages; and some 35 years later, and with more roads beginning to appear on more maps, W. Hollar's chart of Norfolk's roads picked out Brandon–Swaffham–Holkham, Thetford–Attleborough–Norwich, Diss–Norwich, King's Lynn–Brisley–Norwich, King's Lynn–Swaffham, Norwich–Aylsham–Cromer, Norwich–Worstead–Cromer, and Norwich–Loddon–Yarmouth.

By 1663 it was clear that those who actually used the roads, and who needed the improvements, would be the people who would have to pay for them, and in 1663 there was a further important Parliamentary Act. It provided for the repair of highways within the counties of Hertford, Cambridge and Huntingdon (on the line of the Great North Road) and for the introduction of tolls.

Tolls were not a completely new idea. They were relatively common particularly on bridges throughout the Middle Ages, and were collected for a brief period in 1346 for repairs to routes around Charing Cross, St Giles and Temple Bar. However, the country's first proper tollgates of this new road type were finally constructed at Wadesmill, Stilton and Caxton.

For a time, Norfolk, where the roads generally were actually in better condition than many other places, tended to take something of a back seat. In one example, in 1654 John Ogilby recorded that the King's Lynn to Norwich road was 'affording a very good way, much open and healthy'. Perhaps in consequence of its reasonable condition, this important east-west connection never was turnpiked throughout its entire length, though certain stretches were improved.

Elsewhere, matters were gathering pace, and the second great age of road building – the Turnpike Age – was beginning to get under way. It was the first serious attempt since the Romans to introduce a national programme of road construction.

The name 'turnpike' derives from the barriers used to close the new roads, the early forms including a hinged horizontal bar adorned with spikes, or 'pikes', and designed to swing vertically. In consequence, the person in charge became known as the 'pikeman'. Later versions saw the barriers develop into bars or gates designed to swing laterally.

In the event, by about 1700 seven Turnpike Trusts had been created in various parts of the country, and the rate of creation slowly quickened throughout the 18th century until, during the final decade, Acts were going through

The Unicorn coach ran between Norwich and Cromer. The artist would have us believe it travelled a lot faster than was probably the case!

Parliament at the rate of 50 a year. The movement was further assisted by the General Turnpike Act of 1773, which drew attention to the impossibility of maintaining 'through routes' while local variations still existed, and just as important, which extended provision for money to be raised by taxation for the repair of roads.

The toll system was generally unpopular, and had a fragile life. The pikes were a constant challenge for travellers – including most drovers and their herds – who disliked the hard surfaces, or who simply wanted to avoid paying the dues. In one single example of deviousness, people journeying to Norwich from the Coltishall area are said to have avoided the Crostwick toll by turning off the turnpike at Horstead and going through Frettenham or Spixworth. Some of the the barriers even provoked riots. In 1839–44 tempers spilled over in an impoverished area in south-east Wales, sparking what became known as the Rebecca Riots. Toll-bars were torn down and pikemen's houses destroyed.

In addition, some of the pikemen were corrupt, taking bribes to pass traffic through unlawfully or pocketing a proportion of the receipts. Money troubles were never far away from the turnpike system.

Nevertheless, it duly became a worthwhile evil, and by and large the tolls had the required effect. On the whole the remarkable improvement to the general road network seen in the 18th and 19th centuries can be attributed to the tolls. As early as 1698 Celia Fiennes was able to note: 'Thence I went to Windham . . . mostly on a causey, the county being low and morrish and the road on the causey was in many places full of holes, tho' it is secured by a barr at which passengers may pay a penny a horse in order to the mending of the roads, for all about is not to be rode on unless in a dry summer.'

After an early start, however, the progress of improvements in Norfolk began to slow down. There was a gap of over a hundred years, for example, between the construction of the stretch of turnpike near Wymondham mentioned by Celia Fiennes and the opening of the Fakenham turnpike. Again, some of the main roads never were turnpiked, and others were turnpiked only in part.

One reason seems to have been that the general quality of the county's main roads had remained relatively good. In 1794 Nathaniel Kent reported to the Board of Agriculture that the roads in Norfolk were better 'in their natural state, than in almost any other country; so good, that no turnpike was thought of in Norfolk till they became common in other parts'.

The oldest turnpike in Norfolk, and in some ways one of the oldest in Britain, was the stretch between Wymondham and Attleborough. It was placed on the statute book in 1695 at about the same time as the draining of Besthorpe Mere resulted in a slightly more direct route between the two. The Attleborough Road, along with the Harwich Road and the Great North Road, was licensed by the first Turnpike Act, but the Great North Road was actually built first.

On its recently created site in a cul-de-sac near Besthorpe, not far from the new line of the A11, The Dial pillar monument has an inscription dating the bequest of money towards the construction of the road, by Sir Edwin Rich, in 1675. However, the surveyors had to wait some time before they could begin construction, for the actual Act was not passed for another 20 years. The Dial pillar, so called because it once had a sundial on top, was restored in 1888 and again in 1983.

The Attleborough Dial turnpike stone, drawn before restoration.

So most turnpikes did come late to Norfolk, and most roads in the county – perhaps over 90 per cent – never were turnpiked, though a few existing roads were improved by local private landowners.

The bulk of Norfolk's turnpikes were created during the 18th century, but it was a piecemeal process. Two main clusters of roads used Norwich and King's Lynn as their focal points, though there was no completely turnpiked link between the two. However, the pikes to Fakenham and Langor Bridge (a short distance south-east of Little Walsingham) did provide a continuous link. There were also connections for places such as Grimston, Gayton, Fincham, New Buckenham, Bixley, Yaxham, Downham Market, Wells, Thetford, Cromer, Yarmouth and Wisbech. Commercial necessity and local money and influence plainly fuelled some of the schemes and influenced decisions about some of the others.

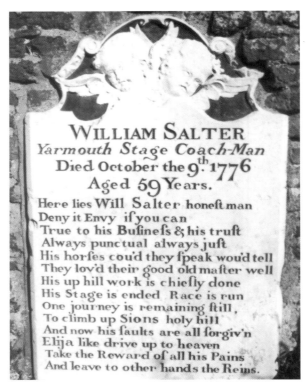

Outside Haddiscoe churchyard.

One branch of the East Dereham turnpike which ran to Mattishall had a clause which said that feather-boards had to be erected to prevent horses being frightened by the Honingham waterwheel.

Dates relating to some of the Norfolk turnpikes – which in general had metalled surfaces made from rammed gravel or stones – include:

Wymondham to Attleborough, 1695
Hethersett to Wymondham, 1708
Attleborough to Larlingford, 1746–47
Norwich to Hethersett, 1746–47
King's Lynn to Downham Market, 1765
Norwich to Scole, 1768
Norwich to Yarmouth (via Blofield, Ormesby, Caister), 1769
Norwich to Dereham, 1770
Norwich to Swaffham, 1770
Norwich to Watton, 1770
Norwich to New Buckenham, 1772
Norwich to Holt, 1784
King's Lynn to Wisbech, 1786
Thetford to Newmarket, 1788
King's Lynn to Thetford, 1792
Norwich to Aylsham, 1794
Norwich to North Walsham, 1796
Aylsham to Cromer, 1811
Norwich to Fakenham, 1823
Wells to Fakenham, 1826
King's Lynn to Fakenham, 1828

As already suggested, the general unpopularity of the toll system tended to obscure its achievements. It is clear, for example, that the advent of improved metalled surfaces provided enormous impetus to a burgeoning coaching industry which, for perhaps the first time, provided the means to enable people to travel regularly over much greater distances and at higher speeds than ever before.

This change of pace also helped to turn the walker, as opposed to the coach traveller or horse rider, into a sort of 'second class citizen' inasmuch as the coach or horse traveller invariably received priority service from an expanding and competitive inn and tavern trade. The assumption was that someone arriving by coach had more spending power than someone on foot.

The turnpikes, and the money raised by the tolls, also helped to establish a proper countrywide network of improved roads by slowly turning a multiplicity of what, in some cases, had been muddy tracks into a system of single routes.

It was the development, spread and popularity of the railways which finally brought an end to the stagecoach era and at the same time wrecked the tolls system. By the mid-1800s, and with the population at large switching to this new, exciting and cheap method of transport, many of the Turnpike Trusts simply went bankrupt.

In 1869 a House of Commons committee considered the Norfolk group and decided that New Buckenham, Norwich, Swaffham and Mattishall, Norwich and Watton, and Thetford, should be discontinued, but that the Aylsham and Cromer Trusts ought to continue for a little longer. One of the last of the Norfolk trusts, the Wells and Fakenham, was dissolved in 1881. Nationally, the last one was wound up in 1895.

Sacred
To the Memory of
JOHN FOX
who on the 20. of Dec.! 1806
in the 79th Year of his Age was
unfortunately kill'd near this spot
having been thrust down & trampled
on by the Horses of a Waggon Tho
his Life was humble yet is it deserving
of imitation He was a worthy & useful
Member of Society an honest
& industrious Labourer
READER
If thou drivest a team be careful
& endanger not the Life of
another or thine own

Memorial at Colney church

Reconstruction of a scene at the tollhouse at Etling Green.

Tollhouses, tollgates, and bridges

Norfolk possessed a large number of tollhouses, though very few remain. The only surviving tollhouse of the Swaffham turnpike is at Etling Green, though it has been much altered externally in recent years. The best example of all, perhaps, is the restored tollhouse at Wiggenhall Magdalen.

If Faden's map of 1797 is to be trusted on the subject, then at that time Norfolk possessed about 40 tollgates, though the overall figure is thought to have been considerably higher.

In 1811 tolls on the Norwich–Aylsham–Cromer turnpike included: coaches (one to six horses) 3*d* to 1*s* 3*d*; waggon (one to four horses) 3*d* to 8*d*; cattle 8*d* per score; sheep and pigs 4*d* per score. By 1834 the St Benedict's (Norwich) tollgate, which extracted tolls from users of the Norwich to Swaffham road, was charging 3*d* for a coach, landau, barouche, gig and hearse; 4*d* for a wain; and 10*d* a score for cattle.

The former tollhouse at Bawdeswell.

The old toll bridge at Guist with (inset right) the modern replacement built alongside, reconstructed in 2005.

A toll bridge, unlike a turnpike road, was usually a commercial concern and belonged to a proprietor or company which would make a profit and pay a dividend, unlike a turnpike road, which was a public highway managed for the public by trustees or commissioners. Indeed, toll bridges were still being built as late as the mid-19th century. One from this period is Ten Mile Bank Bridge at Hilgay, which was built with a tollhouse at the east end.

In the Middle Ages, the western hundred of Norfolk was named Freebridge Hundred because it had a toll free bridge over the river Great Ouse, possibly the one at Wiggenhall Magdalen.

Milestones

The Turnpike Trusts reintroduced milestones, and the first since the days of the Romans was erected on the Dover to Canterbury road in 1663. Slowly the idea spread, and some landowners set up milestones to guide visitors to their estates. Benefactors also donated milestones to their local communities, one such being the 18th-century Holt Obelisk, which was once a gatepost at Melton Constable Hall. Its twin was given to East Dereham, and it remained there until the order to remove signposts during the Second World War was taken somewhat too literally. A set of milestones connecting the two still remains.

Milestones: (left) on the Holt–Dereham road; (right) on the Holt–Cromer road. Both are examples of 'sets' of stones installed during the creation of new roads in the 18th century.

The monumental milestone at Acle Green, erected to mark Queen Victoria's Jubilee.

There are also several milestones, now listed, around Blicking Hall, giving the distance from the Hall to various places, and also one at the old south gates of Felbrigg.

But the heyday of milestones was the turnpike era. For example, an Act of Parliament of 1767 made the trustees of the Thetford and Norwich turnpike responsible for the erection of milestones and signposts, and many of Norfolk's ancient milestones were placed in position in the following hundred years or so.

East Dereham turnpike milestone

The Dereham turnpike still retains its stones with metal plaques at several places. Another stone, in the market place, had as its original inscription, 'London 100 miles, Dereham 0', which seems to have indicated a bit of town pride, perhaps at about the time of the 18th-century rebuilding of the market. Alas, the 'Dereham 0' part of the lettering has been missing for many years.

On Milestone Lane at Wicklewood is another 'London 100 miles' milestone, perhaps related to an estate coaching link between Kimberley Hall and Attleborough and the road to London. This stone has been restored and cared for by a local resident for some years. Milestones on the Norwich to New Buckenham road also carried the distance to London, and there is also one here which proclaims, 'London 100 miles', the reason being that travellers from Norwich to London were directed to New Buckenham and Attleborough, presumably to syphon traffic off the A11 turnpike.

On the road north out of Downham Market, at Cannon Square, is a milestone which is inscribed, 'End of the Lynn Southgate Turnpike Trust'. Another interesting example, on the Green at Acle, is actually a monument erected to mark Queen Victoria's Jubilee.

About 300 milestones of various dates – many from the later County Council period – are thought to remain in Norfolk, some having survived precautionary war-time removals in 1940. Many stones collected from within the boundaries of Norwich were destroyed in 1942 when a bomb struck a council depot in Heigham Street.

Maps and charts

Although the first maps in Britain were produced as early as 1250, the first detailed county maps did not put in an appearance until the late 16th century. Christopher Saxton produced a series of English and Welsh counties in an atlas of 1579, while Camden published his *Britannia* in 1607. Then John Speed produced a popular 'pocket' atlas.

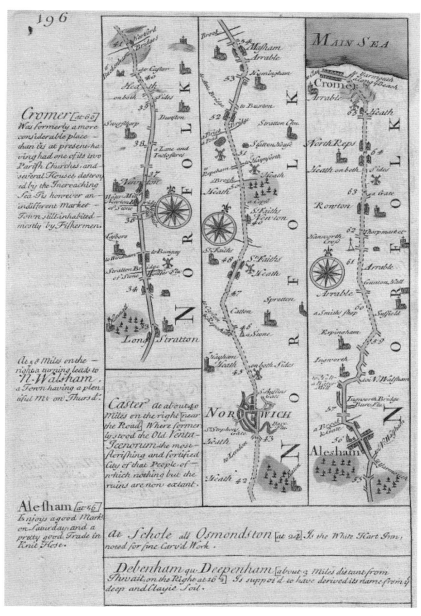

A page from Owen's New Book of Roads, *showing the route from Norwich to Cromer.*

By the mid-18th century details of local roads and local topography were available to wealthy visitors from abroad, but it was the growth of coaching which provided the greatest impetus to the cartographic industry.

John Ogilby, who invented a machine to measure each statute mile, produced an important series of maps in 1675 which ran through many editions, and which was not truly superseded until 1771, when Paterson's work appeared. The 16th edition of Paterson, in 1822, was edited by E. Mogg whose name was placed on subsequent editions. Between 1805 and 1827, Owen's *New Book of Roads* also became a serious competitor in the map market.

As far as Norfolk was concerned, an early important contribution was made by William Faden, geographer to George III, who published a map of the county in 1797. A team of surveyors worked in the county for over four years, and the sheets themselves were more than three years in preparation. Faden's map has proved invaluable to historians, for it portrayed the county on the cusp of change prior to the parliamentary enclosures. Andrew Bryant's county map of 1836 showed Norfolk after some of the enclosures had been completed.

The Board of Ordnance – precursor of the Ordnance Survey – was given the job of producing county maps largely for military purposes because of a threat of invasion from France in the late 18th century. Some one-inch charts were produced, though a difficulty with triangulation was encountered in Norfolk because of a natural shortage of high places. Various printings of Norfolk were made from about 1838 through to 1890, the latter being a composite which included the railway revisions. A national one-inch series was not completed until 1873.

Rural revolution

During the 18th and 19th centuries the growth of industry and an improving prospect of work in the cities and towns contributed to the gradual depopulation of the countryside. Suddenly, there was a need to reorganise agriculture, ostensibly along 'industrial' lines.

Norfolk during the closing years of the 18th century was still a maze of tracks linking isolated farms and settlements, but change came remarkably quickly. In all, during the 18th and 19th centuries, over 300 Parliamentary Enclosures were enacted in the county, involving some 400,000 acres, representing about 30 per cent of its land area.

Sometimes it was simply a process of 'tidying up' particular areas following the abandonment of open field agriculture. Nevertheless, the Commissioners divided the designated land into compact holdings in what was supposed to be a fair and even handed way. Inevitably, it led to disputes.

Part of the enclosure map for Tunstead, showing the northern tip of the parish. The old system of farming open fields is enshrined in the allocation of long, narrow strips to individual owners, whilst bigger landowners are given ownership rights over larger pieces of land. New public roads are created between these parcels of land which had previously been unenclosed. (Norfolk Record Office: PD 285/30)

ROADS AND TRACKS

Waste land and commons were enclosed, marshes drained, scrub cleared and woodland felled. In this way internal field divisions were amended and encased in a framework of new, straight roads.

All this, and, in particular, the loss of a great deal of common land, also contributed to a large amount of rural poverty and further added to the process of rural depopulation and the drift of the masses towards the industrial towns and cities.

Enclosure was achieved in three ways: by Act of Parliament, by order of Commissioners with powers to make awards, and by local consent. Private enclosure Acts were costly, so it was the awards system which was to exert the greatest influence on the road network.

Whereas the old roads ran around ponds, trees and obstacles, following for the most part the old trails, many of the new roads were like a rigid framework. An obvious step was to shorten and straighten the by-roads, but it was pointed out that many of the by-roads had begun life as boundary lines. So ways were found around the land charters.

Where the rectangular fields of Parliamentary Enclosure replaced open field strips, new roads were needed to connect the new holdings with the existing road network. The new roads often followed the geometry of the new boundaries, though they were sometimes poorly connected. One reason was that it was not a continuous process. The enclosure of adjacent parishes might have been a decade apart.

Some new roads did respect ancient boundaries and eccentricities. Again, not every enclosure road was absolutely straight and not every enclosure field was of regular symmetrical proportions; but in general the Commissioners grouped the fields compactly around the new houses. In the space of perhaps two generations the Midlands, in particular, were transformed.

At last long distance coaches could pass through populated areas quickly and safely, and towns and facilities sprang up beside the new routes. It was all a far cry from the days of the gig and light cart, when town roads were repaired with silt from pits dug at convenient distances, when open drains ran through market places, when crossing a road in winter was next to an impossibility, and when stepping stones, wooden posts and railings were familiar street furniture.

Typical of an enclosure road is this long, straight stretch between Fulmodestone and Hindolveston in the north of the county.

There are many examples of enclosure roads in Norfolk; if you see a straight road and straight field boundaries, then you may be very close to one. The roads over Swaffham Heath, from Swaffham to Marham, are one example. Another, the roads which run across the old areas of Mousehold Heath north-east of Norwich – otherwise the Salhouse Road and the South Walsham Road. Built about 1820, they replaced winding tracks. Yet more examples are the roads which run from the A11 to Spooner Row, and from Spooner Row to New Buckenham.

The early part of the 19th century saw other road construction projects accelerate. In 1831 two important new routes opened, the Acle New Road to Yarmouth, and Walpole Cross Keys to Long Sutton over the presently defunct but still visible Sutton Bridge embankment. Its opening, watched by large and excited crowds, immediately forged a safer, shorter and faster link with Lincolnshire and the Midlands. Previously, Wash guides had been needed to take parties across the estuary; otherwise, travellers faced a lengthy detour through Wisbech.

Drove roads

As far as Norfolk is concerned, long distance droving, and thus the use of 'drove' roads or 'driftways', came into being long before the turnpike period, and despite the improvements and the new surfaces on offer the drovers simply continued to use the old routes. Perhaps the main reasons why the turnpikes were not popular with cattlemen was that the cattle did not like the hard surfaces and the drovers did not like paying the tolls. To the drovers, the turnpikes represented a slow and expensive form of travel, and they were certainly no improvement on the older routes they had used for decades.

Like the pilgrims before them, the drovers and their herds also produced a need for facilities such as overnight grazing, lodging and refreshment. At its peak it represented a considerable industry with thousands of head of cattle and sometimes geese being moved across the country or from farms and pastures to the markets.

In the 1840s Scottish cattle, particularly from the Dumfries area, were driven to East Norfolk and re-fattened on the marshes. Their route into Norfolk seems to have been through Wisbech and Setchey. The herds would

This 'drift' or driftway, in Barney, was a short, local drove road – a way along which villagers drove their livestock from the village farm buildings to the pasture outside the confines of the village itself.

then meet up again at the Brick Kiln Inn, Little Plumstead, to prepare for the joint march to London. Herds also assembled at Horsham St Faith, and at the Bird In Hand, Tasburgh, now called The Countryman.

However, the long distance trade began to die in the mid and late 19th century, when the railways came. One example is that of the Bird In Hand at Tasburgh. In 1845 some 9,300 beasts were assembled here; in 1846, the number was twelve. The reason was that the railway had opened that year. The effect was widespread, and in consequence many of the drovers' inns, some of necessity in remote places, slowly perished.

Although no specific drove roads are known in Norfolk, Faden's map uses the word 'drove' in the names of several roads. The road leading out of the bottom of this photograph, going south from Terrington St John, he labels as becoming 'Terrington Drove'.

No specific drove roads are known in Norfolk, though some of today's lanes and tracks were undoubtedly used during the 18th and 19th centuries for long distance cattle droving and the short distance driving of sheep and cattle to the livestock markets.

Stonebreakers and pickers

Sometimes working in gangs, and sometimes simply a lonely figure with his pick and hammer squatting by the roadside, stonebreakers helped keep the roads in trim for decades, particularly from the end of the turnpike era through to the arrival of mechanical tarring. Repairs were often carried out at the whim of the parish council or a local landowner who realised that the collection of stones and the filling of potholes, together with a constant supply of cheap labour, made it a useful maintenance method.

It is recorded that on the then unmetalled way between Swaffham and Cockley Cley gangs of women and boys were employed in the fields as stone pickers. They evidently gathered the stones in bottomless baskets which, when removed, left piles of stones ready to be gathered and used on the roads.

Stone-breakers, depicted by George Walker in his book on The Costumes of York-shire, *published in 1814.*

Lanes, Trains and Cars

The search for the provision of improved roads and metalling actually gained impetus through the expertise of two Scots, Thomas Telford (born 1757) and John Loudon McAdam (born 1756). Telford, a respected engineer, insisted that his roads had substantial foundations of stone blocks and surfaces of graded stones, which were then crushed into a smooth surface by the actions of passing horses and waggons. McAdam's methods were cheaper. He dispensed with expensive foundations, but also believed in layers of graded materials which subsequently, and through use, compacted to provide reasonably waterproof surfaces. There remained, however, the problem of dust.

For a long time the inconvenience remained. Coach passengers sometimes had to wear goggles, while some parishes provided roadside pumps and regular road watering services. In 1845, for example, the Norwich and Thetford turnpike trust erected six pumps, one of which remains to this day at Cringleford, albeit on a slightly different location, and which is now a listed building. It was used to lay dust on the road, though another source, Agar's *Wymondham Old and New*, insists these particular pumps were for filling stone troughs, presumably for the benefit of passing animals. Perhaps they were used for both purposes.

The real challenge, however, was to find a durable substance which would protect road surfaces from mud in winter and dust in summer, for the problem soon began to affect official and commercial enterprises. By 1841 the Royal Mail was being carried by rail rather than by coach, and by 1850 many of the old coaching inns had closed, their yards by now being littered with the debris of the discarded coaches.

So the search for a solution to the dust problem went on, and it caught the imagination of at least one famous writer. In 1899 H. G. Wells, in his prophetic novel *The Sleeper Awakes*, prophesied that a rubber-based substance he called Eadhamite would eventually be used for road surfacing. Wells also forecast that railway lines would eventually be relaid as roads. Wrong in several matters, he was nevertheless nearly right about Eadhamite, for as the search continued first water was used and discarded, and then, following on some American experiments, oil. But even this drastic attempt did not work in damp and muddy England. Then in about 1907 a mixture of hot tar and chipping was found to be the most effective material.

Some forty years earlier another problem had also arisen. The Locomotive and Highways Act of 1865 set a speed limit for the new-fangled steam vehicles of 4 mph in the country and 2 mph in towns. One person had to stoke the engine, another had to steer, while a third was required to walk 60 yards ahead carrying a red flag. The reasoning was sound. It was deemed that an early warning of the presence of such an engine on the road would enable horsemen to take evasive action before their animals bolted from fright. The concept was ridiculed, but it remained on the statute books for thirty years, overlapping into the era of the combustion engine.

Another new contraption seen on the highways was quickly named the Boneshaker, and with good reason. The Boneshaker had wooden wheels and iron tyres. But the bicycle soon became popular, and improved models came on to the market. The Safety, which appeared in the 1880s, had rubber tyres and the general appearance of a modern bicycle. Thus it was that cyclists, and the new cycling clubs, also joined the growing clamour for better surfaces.

However, an even more powerful lobby was soon to make an appearance. In 1888 Edward Butler introduced the first English petrol-driven engine capable of being attached to a moving vehicle, and in 1895 Frederick Lanchester built the first English four-wheeled car. Then in 1896 the Red Flag Act was repealed, and the speed limit raised from 4 mph to 14 mph.

A few months later, in January, 1897, Howes Brothers of Norwich introduced a motor car, a Victoria, to the streets of the city, ostensibly 'to familiarise citizens and horses with the new form of transport'. A few days later a second vehicle was introduced, the experiment – despite the cobbled and uneven streets – being deemed a success. A great future for the vehicle was promptly predicted.

ROADS AND TRACKS

In 1888/89 new administrative units called county councils assumed responsibility for the care of the more important roads and bridges. Norfolk County Council promptly inherited 823 miles of main roads and 267 bridges, a figure which soon grew; many of the bridges were in a crumbling condition and quite inadequate for the new wave of transport and machine vehicles including steam rollers and steam threshing machines. By 1910 the county council had 1400 miles of main roads to protect.

Three years later it was employing 700 men, dozens of horses and three steam tractors. It also maintained the condition of the major roads by a system of roadmen who worked for a number of miles on each side of their place of residence. Other public roads and lanes, however, relied on nearby farmers and landowners for their upkeep. Farmers sometimes dug their own pits to obtain gravel for this purpose.

In the early 1900s – after experiments with mixtures of tar, gravel and much rolling had finally produced solid and level surfaces free of dust – central government made grants to local authorities for the good of the road system. The need was certainly there.

A team of Norfolk County Council road-menders in the centre of Reepham in the early 1900s.

Lanes which were once well used tracks between settlements, such as this one at Northrepps, are often referred to as green lanes. Today many remain open as public bridleways.

Green lanes

Some green lanes or 'soft lanes' are undoubtedly of great antiquity, and they were once a vibrant and vital ingredient in our communications system and our rural heritage. So those fragments which survive today, which are in general among the 'white roads' on Ordnance Survey maps – or the 'white roads with red dots' if recent 1:50,000 maps are taken into account – represent only a tiny proportion of the unmetalled lanes which once existed.

In their 1976 return to the Ministry of Transport, Norfolk listed about 10,250 miles of roads of all kinds in the county, perhaps a third of all these public roads being untarred. This is one clue as to their present state. Those roads and lanes which were not tarred in the early part of the 20th century often simply remained as green lanes.

The origins and dating of most of them remain obscure. A few may even pre-date ownership of the land, and some may have survived because they still represent field or parish boundaries. In the main, however, green lanes are simply unmade roads. Of course, prior to the early part of the century all non-major roads were, in a sense, green lanes. Earlier still, physical boundaries (fences, trees, hedges) became essential to prevent animals straying, and many were built or planted as the surrounding countryside was enclosed. This is one reason why lane boundaries were often deemed the responsibility of the landowner.

Further depletion of this type of road was to come, however. The Country-side Act of 1968 reclassified Roads Used as Public Paths (RUPPs), but as no time limit was set many still survive. The legislative and legal situation is complicated, but RUPPs should not be confused with 'soft lanes', otherwise unsurfaced roads with public vehicular rights, which still remain. Nevertheless, some lanes and sections of lanes have disappeared, largely through incorporation into adjacent fields. However, some fragments survive as field entrances and boundaries.

The survivors have become important wildlife corridors and also create pleasant walking environments. They also provide a glimpse of what rural communications were generally like over periods of hundreds of years. Now neglected, sparsely researched and largely forgotten, green lanes did, nevertheless, provide generations of country people a means of travelling from one town or village to another, and backwards and forwards to work.

Patterns of travel

The increase in travel, encouraged by the railways, was supplemented in the early 20th century by a new fashion for motor buses. In January, 1900, Frank Morriss, the owner of a King's Lynn motor and cycle store, built a motor omnibus to his own design and began a passenger service, largely between South Gates and the Swan Inn at Gaywood. The bus was uphol-stered and the fare was one penny between stopping places, or two pence between Gaywood and the Gates.

The development of passenger carrying transport was boosted by a number of factors, including the railway strike of 1919, the sale of redun-dant First World War vehicles which could be adapted for hackney work, and the arrival from America of a light, pnuematic-tyred bus able to carry a limited number of passengers.

The horse-drawn carriage remained a common form of transport well into the twentieth century. Here Henry Broadhurst MP and his party seem to be on their way to a formal gathering.

The haulage industry was also growing, forcing further re-thinks on highway planning, policy and maintenance. In 1902 the proprietors of the *Eastern Daily Press* planned to modernise their newspaper deliveries and duly acquired an American Oldsmobile vehicle. The first seen in Norfolk, it had a maximum speed of 25 mph. At around midnight on the appointed day the driver left St Andrew's Hill, Norwich, loaded with newspapers and headed for Dereham Post Office followed by Swaffham and King's Lynn. After some distance the gearing went wrong and the vehicle, for some reason, would only move backwards. The driver was thus forced to continue the delivery run as far as Swaffham facing in the wrong direction, kneeling on the driving seat, and holding the steering wheel behind him. Lighting was provided by a borrowed oil bicycle lamp. Not unexpectedly, he gave up the journey in Swaffham. King's Lynn had to go without their EDPs that day.

By 1926 the number of passenger vehicle licences had touched 100,000, horse-drawn buses and carriers' carts by now being largely things of the past. It was also at about this time that much of the tarring of the minor roads was carried out. Parish councils submitted lists of roads to be tarred, leaving a certain number of lanes for cattle. It is still possible to see roads with wide, spaced hedges and verges with a one-vehicle width of metalling snaking between them, the old cattle width having been wider than the area for which money was available for tarring.

With the development of the roads came more road accidents – and the local firms who would turn out to rescue you! If you went into a ditch near Wymondham, it would probably be the Semmence breakdown truck that would arrive.

Almost inevitably, the county councils struggled to keep up with the demand for road space.

The car is king

In 1920 a Ministry of Transport appeared on the scene, and in the 1930s, in the process of casting around for new ideas, it began to take notice of the Italian *autostade* and the German *Autobahn* systems, both very efficient and modern compared to England's meandering ways. In 1930/31 Norfolk and the Ministry finally agreed on the structure of the county's trunk road network, and it is this framework, though subsequently much modified, which in essence is the one still in use today.

Several new schemes were proposed (including, in 1930, a Wymondham bypass) and later dropped, but the Norwich outer ring road, one of the first in the country, was built, in part to help relieve local unemployment. By 1936 trunk roads were also the responsibility of the Ministry, and this period saw the building of the Kingston bypass, perhaps Britain's first major new road of modern times.

For only the third time in British history, the road system was beginning to be modified and improved by national planning rather than by haphazard local development.

The demands of the Second World War brought subtle changes to the county's communications network, for between 1935 and 1945 road access to or in the vicinity of airfields, and the Stanford Battle Area, was restricted. In many cases roads previously open to the public were actually closed, one casualty being the pre-War road link between Watton and Thetford. After the war some of these roads were never reinstated or re-opened, and became permanently lost. In other cases (Bodney, Little Cressingham, Marham, Scottow, for example) the war-time diversions were eventually

---

†

TO THE GLORY OF GOD AND IN SACRED MEMORY OF
MURIEL F. J. BIDWELL.
CHORISTER OF THIS CHURCH WHO WAS MORTALLY INJURED BY A MOTOR CAR & ENTERED PARADISE 10ᵀᴴ DEC 1925 AGED 11 YEARS.

THIS TABLET WAS ERECTED BY PARISHIONERS AND FRIENDS

Memorial brass in Rackheath church

Norfolk's earliest 'dual carriageway', a narrow lane between Tunstead and Scottow which had another carriageway added on the other side of the trees to allow lorries to pass in both directions.

improved. As for the Battle Area, the village of Great Hockham, which took the weight of this diversion, had to wait many decades before it gained some relief from the traffic. A short stretch of dual carriageway between Tunstead and Scottow is also most likely a war-time construction which allowed heavy lorries and vehicles better and safer access to RAF Colt-ishall and the nearby Neatishead radio location station.

After the war, major changes in Norwich included the construction of Rouen Road and the western and northern sections of the inner ring road. A southern bypass was also built at King's Lynn. In the 1960s and 1970s many trunk and county roads were improved. Damgate Street and Market Street at Wymondham, and Bridge Street at Thetford, both still trunk roads until the late 1950s, were given short 'relief' roads, though both towns had to wait until the 1990s before they gained an outer bypass. Lynn's eastern bypass was also built, while the 1970s saw a rush of new bypasses in the county, many of them designed to bring urgent traffic relief to increasingly beleagured small towns and villages. With the 1980s came some improve-ments to the A11 (Cringleford) and the A47, while the 1990s were marked by the opening of Norwich's southern bypass.

The popular availability of the car after the 1939–45 war produced an explosion of ownership which in the 1950s began to place the national network under strain once again. Few people anticipated the scale of increase in private vehicle ownership, or the speed with which it happened.

By the early 1950s many of the county's main roads were plainly becoming inadequate. In high summer, for example, holiday traffic from the Midlands and Lincolnshire moving towards Great Yarmouth or the coastal resorts of north-west Norfolk, created enormous queues of cars and coaches between King's Lynn, Gaywood and Hunstanton, and traffic jams each week-end at Lynn, sometimes with tailbacks of ten or twelve miles, reaching Sutton Bridge and Long Sutton.

The Romans knew that new, improved roads generally generated even more traffic. To this concept might be added the realisation that additional traffic also generated demand for more, improved roads. The syndrome certainly had an effect in the 1960s, a decade which saw the beginning of Britain's motorway construction programme.

In addition, a great many bypasses were also built, between the 1950s and the 1980s in particular, representing an attempt to channel through-traffic away from centres of population. The programme altered many transport routes, and in some cases had the effect of reshaping patterns of settlement and development.

Only a few years ago Wendling, Fransham and Necton were on the main A47 (Norwich to King's Lynn) route, and Norwich to London traffic rumbled through the narrow streets of Wymondham and Attleborough. Bypasses also syphoned some of the through traffic away from Swaffham, East Dereham and elsewhere.

One effect is that short, redundant sections of some of the county's former main roads can be seen by the wayside already 'preserved' as lay-bys, gravel dumps, or cul-de-sacs. When the North Tuddenham bypass was constructed it cut off the end of the Dereham bypass, built some ten years previously; this was taken up, and the land restored to Etling Green. Generally, though, very few redundant road sections have actually been dug up to allow the land to be put to another use.

In the second half of the 19th century, during the era of railway mania, the layout of the county's local roads and tracks had to be changed as the rail tracks spread their tentacles across the land. Sometimes an under-bridge

The coming of the railways often made a difference to existing tracks and roads.
A look at a map before the opening of the railway between North Walsham and
Cromer will show this track leading from Lower Southrepps towards Thorpe Market;
the hedge in the background shows the railway blocking the former track.

or over-bridge would be provided for the road, sometimes a level crossing
(even a simple unmanned crossing). Sometimes, however, the decision
was that no such provision was warranted and the road was simply cut and
fell out of use. In places such as West Runton the road had to be rerouted
and an awkward bend in the modern road shows where it diverges from the
original route. A comparison of maps or a good eye for the landscape will
often reveal such changes. However, the second half of the 20th century
would put the situation into reverse.

A drastic reduction of the pre-war railway network occurred in the 1960s, and
many of the disused lines eventually gained other uses, usually as new roads.
This occurred at Holt, East Dereham, Wortwell, North Walsham and Stalham,
and many other places. The swing bridge at Sutton Bridge – the latest of several bridges over the River Nene at this point – once carried a railway line
on one side and a road for motor vehicles on the other. With the conversion
of the old rail line through Cross Keys to a modern trunk road, however,
the bridge has since handled two-way road traffic. Sections of other former
railway lines have become leisure footpaths, including part of the Weavers
Way near Aylsham and Marriotts Way near New Costessey and Drayton.

This photograph is taken from just north of where Gorleston North station once stood. The line of the railway, opened in 1903 by the Norfolk and Suffolk Joint Railway company and closed in 1942, is now followed by the busy dual carriageway for the A12 through Gorleston.

The beginning of the 21st century has seen another attempt to unblock the great jams that we have already referred to as the traffic from the Midlands attempts to get round the corner and into Norfolk, with the construction of the large roundabout and intersection south-east of King's Lynn. Other developments are linked to major building development, such as the link road that now provides access from Thickthorn to the Norfolk and Norwich University Hospital.

As the century moves onwards, decisions on the future of the county's roads are often a considerable topic of debate. Indeed, the retention of the very land itself has been thrown into contention as we consider just how much can be defended against the encroaching sea. An option for allowing the sea to flood inland across part of the Broads would certainly see a major change in the road layout in the north-east of the county, and even perhaps raised roads of the type found in the Florida Keys. Old maps show where roads once ran at places like Sidestrand and Paston, until the cliff slipped and a new line had to be established, so there is a precedent, albeit on a much smaller scale.

The concern for the environment and a certain quality of life has led to the development of new tracks. Localised development, such as the boardwalk across Southrepps Common or those created as part of the Coastal Path, meets the needs of walkers, whilst both pedestrians and cyclists benefit from roads now designated 'Quiet Lanes'. The development of the Peddars Way and the Coastal Path as part of the Long Distance Footpath mix both traditional tracks and recently established footways.

At the other end of the scale is the continuing demand for more dualling of the A11, with the original track both widening and sometimes shifting its line as part of that process. The question of the dualling of the A47, particularly to the east of Norwich, remains a vexed question with two very different points of view expressing their demands. The line of a possible northern bypass for Norwich has been the subject of much paperwork and public consultation.

One of the areas that could see the most change in the 2010s is that around Great Yarmouth, as part of the 1st East proposals. The success of the outer harbour is likely to be dependent on improving the structure of the supporting road network. The most significant element of this is likely to be a further river crossing, in the form of the proposed Nelson Bridge. In the same way that the railway and then the road gradually tried new lines of approach to the town, greatly changing the old approach from the north through the Fleggs, the new bridge is intended to shift the main town entrance further south, enabling the harbour service area to operate on the south half of the spit and other residential and appropriate quayside developments in areas which are currently industrial.

In all this, Norfolk still does not possess a single metre of motorway and main routes have not been dualled in their entirety. It remains to be seen if the third great age of road building is coming to an end; there are signs, some financial and some environmental, that this may be so.

Index